ROBERT DE MOOR

GOD'S BACKYARD

A FRESH LOOK AT ECCLESIASTES

CRC Publications
Grand Rapids, Michigan

Acknowledgments

We are grateful to Paul Stoub, a free-lance artist from Grand Rapids, Michigan, for the illustrations that grace this text and bring the images to life.

Unless otherwise indicated, the Scripture quotations in this publication are from the Holy Bible, New International Version. Copyright © 1973, 1978, 1984 International Bible Society. Used by permission of Zondervan Bible Publishers.

❀ Printed in the United States of America on recycled paper.

Library of Congress Cataloging-in-Publication Data
De Moor, Robert, 1950-
God's backyard: a fresh look at Ecclesiastes/Robert De Moor.
    p. cm.
ISBN 1-56212-038-7
1. Bible. O.T. Ecclesiastes—Commentaries. I. Title.
BS1475.3.D46 1993
223' .807—dc20   93-27782
CIP

10 9 8 7 6 5 4 3 2 1

Contents

Preface

People are again asking questions about the meaning and purpose of human existence. They wonder:

• Why was I placed in this world?
• What's the point of my life?
• Where am I going and why?
• Is this trip worth taking?

Recent world changes and sliding ethical values have made these questions sharper and more urgent.

These are also the questions of Ecclesiastes. The author of this Old Testament book calls himself "The Teacher, son of David, king in Jerusalem." But although he is the Teacher, he gives no easy answers. Rather he sets the great life questions in their proper context, as the queries of a person who recognizes that there is a God who sets limits for "everything under the sun." It is only by respecting those divine limits that we can ask sensible questions and discover wise answers.

The author of *God's Backyard*, Rev. Robert De Moor, takes a fresh look at this often misunderstood and underappreciated book. He shows that this is no treatise in secular philosophy that somehow happens to have gotten into the Bible. The "backyard" of De Moor's title is God's

world. We are the Lord's little children, free to explore that yard as long as we recognize the One who sits like a wise Grandfather at the window watching our play and as long as we respect the fences that enclose our play space.

The twelve chapters of this book take us through the thoughts of the Teacher from the beginning statement, "'Meaningless! Meaningless!' says the Teacher. 'Utterly meaningless! Everything is meaningless'" to the concluding "Fear God and keep his commandments, for this is the whole duty of man." They show us the wisdom of a person who both lives and questions life before the face of God.

Robert De Moor is a pastor, presently serving the First Christian Reformed Church of Langley, British Columbia. This is his fourth pastorate, all in the Alberta or British Columbia area.

Also available is a leader's guide to aid you in using this book in study-group situations. This guide was developed by Dennis De Groot, vice-principal and English teacher at the Fraser Valley Christian High School in Surrey, British Columbia.

Harvey A. Smit
Editor in chief
Education Department

5

Fresh Forays to the Fence

The words of the Teacher, son of David, king in Jerusalem.
Ecclesiastes 1:1

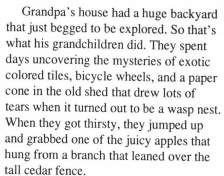

Grandpa's house had a huge backyard that just begged to be explored. So that's what his grandchildren did. They spent days uncovering the mysteries of exotic colored tiles, bicycle wheels, and a paper cone in the old shed that drew lots of tears when it turned out to be a wasp nest. When they got thirsty, they jumped up and grabbed one of the juicy apples that hung from a branch that leaned over the tall cedar fence.

The mystery of the apple-bearing branch hanging there in midair beckoned them to scramble over the fence to find its source, or failing that, at least to gain a glimpse of what lay beyond. But try as they might, they could not reach the top of that fence. The harder they tried, the more frustrated they became. Their strained efforts turned the pleasant summer sun into a searing torch until, discouraged, they returned to their play, wandering around Grandpa's garden, poking at this and that, making do with whatever they could find. And when Grandpa smiled and made faces at them from the upstairs window, they were happy.

Enter Qoheleth

Like a child helping a kid brother or sister explore Grandpa's yard, Qoheleth, the Teacher, invites us along on a tour of God's creation. He invites us "to study and to explore by wisdom all that is done under heaven" (1:13).

We're not here to mow the lawn: plodding along systematically in precise, logical sweeps, never to retrace our steps. Instead, we roam freely with the Teacher, often covering and recovering the same ground, constantly searching and researching; evaluating and reevaluating. And yet, wherever wisdom takes us, we bump into the fence—into the limits that God has placed around our human efforts to achieve, to know, and to understand.

Qoheleth has been here before. Like us, he has tried in vain to climb the fence, to break through the limits God has imposed on "everything under the sun." But his constant failures have finally taught him to respect those limits, to explore only what can be properly explored within the boundaries, and most importantly, to look up at the God who sets them. In retelling the story of his journey, he invites us along on it, so that we too might arrive where he has come:

Now all has been heard; here is the con-
clusion of the matter: Fear God and keep
his commandments, for this is the whole
duty of man.

(12:13)

Who Is He?

We do not know who this teacher was.
His title, Qoheleth, indicates that he
addressed the *Qahal*, the "assembly" of
God's people. (*Qoheleth* translated into
Greek is *Ecclesiastes*, which means
speaker at the "ecclesia" or "gathering.")
He taught rather than preached, so our
best English equivalent might simply be
"Teacher."

We can gather from his book that
Qoheleth was an upper-class, God-fear-
ing Jew who lived in Jerusalem. James L.
Kugel writes:

> He inhabits a world, or more precise-
> ly, a class, of financial high-rollers. In
> that world fortunes are amassed (2:8)
> or lost in a bad business deal (5:14);
> accumulated wealth is managed for
> good or ill (5:12), even sent overseas
> (11:1). There is no talk of petty loans
> to farmers in need of tiding over . . .
> Indeed there is no talk of borrowing or
> loaning at all, nor of its costs: money,
> or rather fortunes, seem to be *invested*
> . . . this suggests a milieu of relatively
> sophisticated financial dealings, and of
> a class of entrenched wealth.
> — *"Qoheleth and Money,"*
> The Catholic Biblical
> Quarterly, *Vol. 51, p. 32f*

Qoheleth was well-educated, but he
was no ivory-tower snob: "Not only was
the Teacher wise, but also he imparted
knowledge to the [common] people"
(12:9). The traditional view has been that
the Teacher was King Solomon himself.

However, this seems unlikely. His writing style is salted with Aramaisms,
Persian and Phoenician loan words, and
types of thought that would place him in
a much later time slot—most likely at the
time the Ptolemaic dynasty ruled
Palestine from Egypt in the third century
B.C. Reinforcing this view is the fact that
the book suggests a relatively stable peri-
od within the history of God's people,
despite their subjection to foreign rule.

Yet, some things in the book undeni-
ably point to Solomon as the author. The
Teacher is "son of David, king in
Jerusalem" (1:1, 12). He has "grown and
increased in wisdom more than anyone
who has ruled over Jerusalem before"
(1:16). He "became greater by far than
anyone in Jerusalem" (2:9). These
descriptions certainly remind us of
Solomon. But nowhere does the anony-
mous scribe who has recorded his teaching specifically identify him as such.
And, as we have seen, the Teacher's language and thought patterns cannot be
placed easily in a time frame as early as
Solomon's.

So what's the solution?

R.N. Whybray suggests in his recent
commentary on Ecclesiastes,

> The fact that [Solomonic authorship]
> is made only indirectly, hinting at the
> identification but never actually nam-
> ing Solomon . . . may suggest that
> Qoheleth never intended his readers to
> take it seriously. In fact, the fiction is
> dropped after chapter two and not
> resumed. . . ."
> —The New Century
> Bible Commentary:
> Ecclesiastes, *p. 4*

So most likely the Teacher was not
Solomon, but, for effect, he put himself

in Solomon's place. Who else had pushed the limits of human achievement and wisdom as far as Solomon had? Where could he find a model better suited for testing the boundaries of what we can amount to under the sun? Without trying to pass himself off as the "real" Solomon, the Teacher invites us to join him in seeing what we can see from Solomon's vantage point, so that we too may become wise.

Comparing Wisdom and Reality

Three sources provide the input for Qoheleth's investigation into what we can discover about God's world.

1. Traditional Wisdom

Qoheleth displays extensive knowledge of Israel's rich treasury of wisdom sayings, which by his time were well-established and time-tested. "He pondered and searched out and set in order many proverbs" (12:9). But rather than simply collecting such sayings, he enters into an ongoing dialogue with them, evaluating and testing them, and often balancing them with other proverbs or observations that sometimes contradict each other. The Teacher appears to be intrigued by the fact that these sayings also have their definite limits—they can only tell one side of the story. So instead of taking traditional wisdom for granted, he constantly interrupts with a "yes, but . . . ."

In taking this approach, Qoheleth follows other writers of his day who became critical of the old wisdom. But he stops short of throwing traditional wisdom on the intellectual junk heap. In it he still hears the voice of his Good Shepherd (12:11).

The older wisdom tradition had positively and optimistically asserted that already in this life God rewards wise, good behavior and punishes the stupidity of the wicked. Qoheleth observes that the real world does not seem to work that way. As often as not, good people die young and the wicked have a ball. How can one explain this ugly mystery?

Qoheleth doesn't. He admits that when he tries to find an explanation, he once again bumps headlong into the fence that God has placed around our ability to know.

Yet, despite its limitations, older, traditional wisdom has much to offer. And Qoheleth gladly makes use of it—sometimes quoting it as gospel truth, at other times raising it as a foil for his own contrary observations.

2. His Own Experience

Combined with his great learning, Qoheleth displays a wealth of personal experience through which he has been able to hone and craft his insights. Whether he is Solomon himself or someone who plays the part, he shows the poignant originality of thought and realism of someone who has been around the block and back.

3. His Knowledge of God.

Qoheleth anchors his investigation in his firm knowledge of and faith in God. This faith clearly shows him the way through what otherwise would be a very bleak and hopeless conclusion. Many commentators have failed to grasp the solidity of that faith, and have consequently branded Qoheleth a disillusioned pessimist.

For example, James Crenshaw writes:

This, then, Qoheleth observes about the human situation. Wisdom's claim to secure one's existence is patently false. No discernible principle of order exists, no heavenly guarantor rewards good conduct and punishes evil deeds. The distant creator, if involved at all, punishes only flagrant affronts such as reneging on religious vows. Since death cancels every imagined gain, rendering life under the sun absurd, one should enjoy a woman, wine, and food before old age and death end even these fleeting pleasures. In sum, Qoheleth examines experience and discovers nothing that will survive death's arbitrary blow.

—The Old Testament Library: Ecclesiastes, *p. 28*

But despite his oft-repeated claim that all is meaningless, Qoheleth nowhere rejects the essential claims of traditional wisdom. He refuses to call his teachers liars. And he is no pessimist. The maturity of his faith gives him the ability to unblinkingly see, accept, and describe reality as it actually is, without sugarcoating any bitter pills. It lends him the courage to dare to be an uncompromising realist, allowing him to challenge the teaching of traditional wisdom, to fill in some of its glaring gaps, and to pose the everyday, gut-wrenching questions that it simply cannot answer.

Qoheleth's trust in God never wobbles. It remains the solid bedrock out of which faith seeks understanding and, failing that, learns to live peaceably with the unanswered question. God knows even if we don't. That's sufficient.

A Sound Still Worth Hearing?

Because Qoheleth does not set up his message in a tidy, easily comprehended package, scholars disagree about what his point really is.

Many, like Crenshaw, see Qoheleth as nothing more than a skeptic, a person who dourly upsets the apple-cart of faith while giving nothing in return. They point to his constant refrain that everything "under the sun" is meaningless and that death will ultimately erase everything. But this view fails to account for Qoheleth's other major refrains:

A man can do nothing better than to eat and drink and find satisfaction in his work. This too, I see, is from the hand of God, for without him, who can eat or find enjoyment? To the man who pleases him, God gives wisdom, knowledge and happiness. . . .

(2:24-26)

Be happy, young man, while you are young, and let your heart give you joy in the days of your youth. Follow the ways of your heart and whatever your eyes see, but know that for all these things God will bring you to judgment. So then, banish anxiety from your heart and cast off the troubles of your body, for youth and vigor are meaningless.

(11:9-10)

These passages seem to breathe a very different spirit than the thoroughly secular, pessimistic works that can be found elsewhere in the Middle East. One such work, translated in *Ancient Near Eastern Texts* by J.B. Pritchard, cites a dialogue between a nobleman and his servant in which the servant cares nothing about truth and is interested only in keeping his head:

"Servant, obey me."

"Yes, my lord, yes."

"The chariot—hitch it up. I will ride to the palace."

"Ride, my lord, ride! The king will be gracious to you."

"No, servant, I shall not ride to the palace."

"Don't ride, my lord, don't ride. The king might send you to some out-landish place. You'd never get a moment's peace."
—Ancient Near Eastern Texts,
p. 438

Similar exchanges take place over such proposed activities as eating, hunting, and romance. Each time the noble-man changes his mind, and the servant, prudently, changes his counsel. Finally, the master asks the philosophical question, "What is good?" And answers it himself: "To break my neck, your neck, throw both in the river—that is good." When the servant refuses to respond, the master changes his mind again, proposing that he shall just break his servant's neck and send him on ahead to the land of the dead. At last he manages to extract from his servant some honest counteradvice: how could his master continue to survive with no one to look after him!

In this dialogue a wise man, like Qoheleth, is also driven to the rainbow's end before stating the truth. But unlike Qoheleth, when he gets there, he finds neither God nor promise to console him. So although they share a common form, these two writings have nothing material-ly in common.

Some Other Views

Others guess that Qoheleth's original message was so thoroughly scandalous and ungodly that a subsequent biblical scribe had to make extensive revisions in order to make it palatable for the average,

pious, God-fearing Jew. This view is now also by and large rejected. It fails to answer a major problem of why a devout scribe would waste his time on such an unorthodox document in the first place, and also why he would make such a transparent mess of it. A wise scribe would have more brains than that!

In one of his lectures on Ecclesiastes, John Stek, former professor of Old Testament theology at Calvin Seminary, identifies still another group of commen-tators who see in Ecclesiastes a call to believers to hang in there, even though the gospel train of God-wrought redemp-tive history has stalled on the tracks. These commentators point to the subse-quent events of Christmas, Easter and Pentecost to show that Qoheleth's mes-sage, while laudable in his own day, would be totally inadequate and inappro-priate now that God is once again on the move in Christ.

Stek proposes a better approach: to view Qoheleth's message as a Holy-Spirit-inspired exploration of the endur-ing creation order by which God holds the world and everything in it in his hand. Regardless of where we find ourselves within redemptive history, our faithful God keeps a grip on reality and maintains the ordinances and statutes that hold it together.

Can wisdom show us what to make of our days and years "under the sun?" Without denying the radical changes brought about in our existence as a conse-quence of God's mighty acts, are there also things that stay the same? Can insight into those permanent boundaries of reality and of our lives help us walk in wisdom's ways in any age, even in our own? This is Qoheleth's quest. The time-less currency and relevance of his search makes it worth our while to tag along on

his meandering tour through Grandpa's
backyard.

CHAPTER TWO

Mega-Meaninglessness

*"Meaningless! Meaningless!"
  says the Teacher.
"Utterly meaningless!
  Everything is meaningless."*

*What does man gain from all his labor
  at which he toils under the sun?
Generations come and generations go,
  but the earth remains forever.
The sun rises and the sun sets,
  and hurries back to where it rises.
The wind blows to the south
  and turns to the north;
round and round it goes,
  ever returning on its course.
All streams flow into the sea,
  yet the sea is never full.
To the place the streams come from,
  there they return again.
All things are wearisome,
  more than one can say.
The eye never has enough of seeing,
  or the ear its fill of hearing.
What has been will be again,
  what has been done will be done
    again;
  there is nothing new under the sun.
Is there anything of which one can say,
  "Look! This is something new"?
It was here already, long ago;
  it was here before our time.*

*There is no remembrance of men
  of old,
  and even those who are yet to
    come
will not be remembered
  by those who follow.*

*I, the Teacher, was king over Israel in
Jerusalem. I devoted myself to study and
to explore by wisdom all that is done
under heaven. What a heavy burden God
has laid on men! I have seen all the
things that are done under the sun; all of
them are meaningless, a chasing after the
wind.*

*What is twisted cannot be straightened;
  what is lacking cannot be counted.*

*I thought to myself, "Look, I have
grown and increased in wisdom more
than anyone who has ruled over
Jerusalem before me; I have experienced
much of wisdom and knowledge." Then I
applied myself to the understanding of
wisdom, and also of madness and folly,
but I learned that this, too, is a chasing
after the wind.*

*For with much wisdom comes much sorrow;
  the more knowledge, the more grief.*
—Ecclesiastes 1:2-18

When children play in the backyard, they don't accomplish very much. The overgrown grass and the weeds remain pretty much as they are. The rusted-out bucket ends up in the ditch, and the TV cabinet gets toppled onto its face. Grandpa will have to sneak in someday to clean up the pile of old linoleum and busted two-by-fours that stands as a now-abandoned fort.

Nothing worthwhile really gets accomplished, but so what? We expect that from children.

But not from ourselves.

A Stinging Conclusion

Reenter Qoheleth. He wastes no time at all cutting out from under us our grand illusion that we big people are in any way different than those kids.

"Meaningless! Meaningless!" says the Teacher. "Utterly meaningless! Everything is meaningless."

(1:2)

Not a very pleasant bucket of cold water he throws on us hard-working, responsible adults! But Qoheleth is not interested in pleasantries. He's interested in telling it like it is so that we will face facts. He has to lance one of our dearest misconceptions: that what we accomplish in this world will somehow last and make a real, abiding difference.

In the original Hebrew the word the NIV translates as "meaningless" (*hevel*) literally means "breath." Like our breath on a frosty day, everything we achieve in this world disappears in a puff of air. The psalmists often use the same word to express how fleeting our days really are:

Lowborn men are but a breath, the high-born are but a lie; if weighed on a bal-
ance, they are nothing; together they are only a breath.

—Psalm 62:9

The NIV grasps some of the intent of this word in its translation: "Meaningless." But the term carries even more freight—not only the idea of futili-ty, but also of something disappointingly insubstantial. *Hevel* is like coming home with a ravenous appetite from a hard day in the field to find only a tossed green salad on your plate—so small it wouldn't even hold a rabbit till breakfast! The term also strongly carries that related sense of impermanence, of being here today and gone tomorrow—if it even lasts that long.

Michael V. Fox claims that for Qoheleth the word bears another meaning as well: "absurd."

The essence of the absurd is a dispari-ty between two terms that are sup-posed to be joined by a link of harmo-ny or causality but are, in fact, dis-junct. The absurd is an affront to rea-son, in the broad sense of the human faculty that looks for order in the world about us. The quality of absur-dity does not inhere in a being, act, or event in and of itself . . . but rather in the tension between a certain reality and a framework of expectation.
—*"The Meaning of Hebel for Qohelet,"* Journal of Biblical Literature, *Vol. 105, p. 409*

Essentially the word *hevel* puts into one word Qoheleth's deep disappoint-ment that in a universe where God is master, there seems to be not the slightest connection between what we do and what happens to us. The absence of that con-nection seems to make everything irra-tional and pointless.

To emphasize his own despair at this gruesome discovery, Qoheleth stacks the word on top of itself: "Breath of breaths"—a Hebrew way of emphasizing the utmost extreme of something. Just as "the king of kings" refers to the most exalted king and the "song of songs" to the greatest song, so "the breath of breaths" expresses the height of meaninglessness, absurdity, transitoriness. Fox observes, "The individual absurdities are not anomalies. Their absurdity infects the entire system, making 'everything' absurd" ("The Meaning of Hebel for Qohelet," pp. 426-427).

Using a contemporary idiom (with its tendency to mix metaphors), we might simply translate verse 2: "Mega-meaningless. The whole shootin' match amounts to a God-forsaken hill of beans." Such a lack of connection between our actions and any predictable or lasting consequence becomes Qoheleth's wail of despair to the Almighty, who allows this irrational state of affairs to exist everywhere and in every time.

To drive home this major theme, Qoheleth elaborates on it in a poem (1:3-11) before fleshing out for us the way he arrives at his terrifying conclusion (1:12-15).

An Unprofitable Business

In his poem, Qoheleth takes us for a very quick spin around the entire backyard in order to show us the lay of the land. Later he will show us more detail. For now he frames this first survey by beginning and ending it with his primary concern: humanity and what we can and cannot do. He reminds us that he's not interested in detached, theoretical philosophizing about the nature of reality. His search is intensely concrete and practical. What does it all mean to *us*? Where can

we fit into this grand scheme of things to find some permanent significance?

But he fails to find any absolute purpose to our struggle. There is nothing we can do that has lasting value (vv. 3-4) or that at the very least would provide future generations with a permanent memory of us (v. 11).

Qoheleth begins by asking, "What does man gain from all his labor at which he toils under the sun?" (1:3). The implied, desperate response: "NOTHING—ZIP!"

The word he uses for *gain* literally means "excess" or "remainder." It's a banking term that refers to the bottom line after one subtracts expenses from income. What's left? A big, fat zero.

How utterly frustrating! After all, we sweat and slave and work our fingers to the bone; twice in this verse he uses a word that means "heavy labor, backbreaking toil." How meaningless that all our strenuous efforts just evaporate into thin air! How brutally absurd and unfair!

Is it all hopeless then, our hard work? And does grasping this reality put us so deeply in the pit of despair that we might as well pack up our tools and quit?

Qoheleth already tips his hand just a wee bit to give us a glimpse of where we might start looking for an answer beyond this cruel reality. To this sigh of deep despair he attaches a phrase he uses often: "What does man gain from all his labor at which he toils *under the sun*?" (1:3). Alternately he uses the equivalent phrase "under heaven" (1:13). By using these phrases he carefully stipulates the limits within which his sobering observations hold true: "under the sun," which means "in this world." In the whole backyard, nothing lasting or permanent gets done. But is the backyard all there is?

Cycles to Nowhere

Later Qoheleth will explain. For now he needs to rub our noses in the unpleasant mess of our own inability. He must take before he can give. He must strip away our naive, youthful idealism and our day-to-day busyness that make us forget the essential truth: "Generations come and generations go, but the earth remains forever" (1:4).

Nothing we do makes any lasting impact. The world just stays the same whether we live or die. Despite our sweat and strain and suffering, "that ol' man river jes' keeps on rollin' along."

Three examples Qoheleth takes from nature drive this home. All of them are endlessly repeating cycles that never change the iron-clad order in which they are fixed.

Qoheleth points to the sun. Day after day it rises and sets, rises and sets. It does its best, but nothing ever changes. It always returns to where it came from. The Hebrew reads: "[the sun] *pants* back to where it rises" (1:5). It's like a lion, who, winded by a fruitless chase, plops back down in its lair exhausted, out of breath, and still hungry.

The wind also demonstrates that everything that goes around comes around, like a dog chasing its own tail:

The wind blows to the south and turns to the north; round and round it goes, ever returning on its course.

(1:6)

Finally, he points to the fact that all the constant, restless activity of rivers and streams to fill the ever-thirsty sea never meet with success:

All streams flow into the sea, yet the sea is never full. To the place the streams come from, there they return again.

(1:7)

This endless activity that spins round and round without getting anywhere tires Qoheleth out. "All things are wearisome, more than one can say" (1:8). He simply cannot find the words.

And just like the sea: "The eye never has enough of seeing, nor the ear its fill of hearing" (1:8).

Talk to any senior with a lifetime of experiences behind her. Hasn't she seen and heard enough? From horse and buggy to lunar rovers. From ragtime to hymn sing. Isn't it enough now? No, it's not enough! The tears well up as she pours out her frustration of wanting to see more, wanting to hear more, but being unable to because she's going blind and deaf. So she strains to read one more page, to hear once more the happy chatter of a favorite grandchild. And when she can't, she tries to remember the happy sounds of long ago, of Christmas carols, of her husband's voice long since silenced in the grave.

But the relentless cycle of generations coming and generations going continues its endless, pondering roll. We work and struggle till we drop. But the world goes on as if we never existed:

What has been will be again, what has been done will be done again; there is nothing new under the sun.

(1:9)

So What's New?

We live in a time of unprecedented change . . . or do we? So automobiles have more than quadrupled our speed in reaching the market. So refrigerators increase the time before we need to go there again. For the most part the world grinds on as it always has. All over the globe we still struggle to make a buck, and when we cannot make ends meet, we get desperate and march into battle for some joker who promises honor and freedom and what we're really after— enough bread to fill our bellies. Sure, video stores have replaced storytellers, newspapers the village busybody, and chemotherapy the old folk medicines. But the rich are still getting richer, the poor are becoming more desperate, and in the end the grave greedily swallows us all. Qoheleth asks:

Is there anything of which one can say, "Look! This is something new?" It was here already, long ago; it was here before our time.

(1:10)

Even our most ingenious inventions and grandest exploits cannot begin to make a dent in the order of things. Not all the "newness" of our age changes the basic facts of life:

Time, like an ever-rolling stream, soon bears us all away; we fly forgotten, as a dream dies at the opening day.
—Psalter Hymnal *1987, 170:5*

The pharaohs of ancient Egypt spent large chunks of their nation's G.N.P. to build themselves overgrown grave markers for when they passed on. Pyramids seemed like a safe bet: solid, massive, impressive, lasting. They are still there today. But the memory of their occupants has long since faded. What's left of their mummified remains lie in plexiglass museum cases exposed to the furtive

peeks of school children who loudly proclaim them to be "totally gross!" King Tut's burial stuff has become a nice little money-maker at $5.50 a pop.

Even the pyramids themselves are decaying. Worse than Napoleon Bonaparte's arrogant act of blowing the nose right off the Sphinx, the air pollution caused by this century's "modernization" of Egypt is gradually grinding these mighty monuments to bits. Sooner or later they will simply melt back into the desert, leaving no trace.

Listen to Qoheleth *before* you sock too much of your cash into a preburial package deal:

There is no remembrance of men of old, and even those who are yet to come will not be remembered by those who follow.

(1:11)

A Heavy Burden

How does Qoheleth arrive at such a disheartening conclusion? He tells us in verses 12-15.

As an ambitious young fellow with everything going for him, he "devoted himself to study and to explore by wisdom all that is done under heaven" (1:13). But his backyard wanderings had a higher goal than idle curiosity. He "wanted to see what was worthwhile for men to do under heaven during the few days of their lives" (2:3). Like all of us, Qoheleth wants his life to have some kind of meaning or purpose. We all need to feel that we have some value. Without a sense of self-worth we're left devastated, even suicidal. Why keep trying if we won't get anywhere anyway? Why endure the darkness when there's no light at the end of the tunnel?

It's not that we need to have everything handed to us on a platter. We'll

work hard. We'll make every sacrifice.
We'll learn and take advice and struggle.
But we need *some* hope of getting somewhere, some inkling that our lives may
have some meaning—otherwise why
should we even bother to get out of bed?

This is precisely Qoheleth's burden.
He'll gladly go the extra ten yards. He'll
give two hundred percent. But everything
he tries is "a chasing after the wind"
(1:14); nothing to grasp, nothing to gain,
nothing he can ever hope to hold onto.
Nothing he does ever makes any difference:

What is twisted cannot be straightened;
what is lacking cannot be counted.
(1:15)

Why, God?

One thing makes Qoheleth feel the
sting of that discovery even more
sharply: it is *GOD* who has laid this burden on us (1:13)!

In a universe without God, we could
live with absurdity, even our own. Why
should things be any different? They just
are. Grin and bear it.

In a universe with many gods, we
might also expect such pointless absurdity. The Greeks have a myth about
Sisyphus, a man who ended up on the
wrong side of a deity or two. He was con-
demned forever to push a rock up a high
mountain. Unfortunately for poor
Sisyphus, the higher he got up the mountain, the bigger and heavier the rock
grew. The harder he tried to get it to the
top, the more spectacularly he failed. And
with every failure, he had to climb all the
way back down, pick up the rock again,
and start over.

In a universe with many gods, we can
expect a few rotten apples in the pan-
theon who delight in torturing a poor

(im)mortal by condemning him to a life
of hopeless futility.

But that's not the universe we live in.
We live in a universe where there is only
one true God. His name is Yahweh, the
great I AM, who always remains true to
his promises, faithful to his people, and
an overwhelming fountain of grace and
love and kindness. Qoheleth, as one of
God's covenant people, knew God well
that way. But that intimate connection
with God gave him all the more reason to
agonize over the ugly mystery that
Yahweh could be so cruel! How can God
lay such a trip on us?

Qoheleth never once calls God by his
covenant name. Instead of *Yahweh*, he
consistently uses the term *elohim*: "God."
This term points to God's absolute sover-
eignty rather than to love, kindness, and
saving grace. In his exploration of what
goes on "under the sun," Qoheleth bumps
into a God who is the all-powerful
Wholly Other, who remains strangely
distant, who condemns all humanity to an
apparently meaningless existence. He
knows that somehow these two sides of
God must come together and dovetail.
But *how*? It's really tough when you look
around the backyard and realize that it's
Grandpa himself who built that stupid
fence!

Wisdom's Grief

Any college kid who has had to "pull
an all-nighter" to cram for an exam can
identify with Qoheleth's complaint that

with much wisdom comes much sorrow;
the more knowledge, the more grief.
(1:18)

The fact that so many other near-
Eastern wisdom writings offer the same
complaint shows that students back then

knew only too well how tough disci-
plined study can be. In fact, they knew it
better. Compounding their sorrow and
grief was the prevailing educational theory in those days that by inflicting harsh
physical punishments—we'd call it "negative reinforcement"—teachers would
provide the motivation their students
needed to maximize their potential.

But Qoheleth's reason for offering this
complaint lies elsewhere. It is precisely
his great learning and wisdom that allow
him to see the painful reality of the empty
meaninglessness of everything that
humans try to achieve. Furthermore, his
learning fails to provide any reasons for
God's placing this heavy burden on us.
Even the pursuit of wisdom itself proves
to be a fruitless effort; it also turns out to
be nothing more than "a chasing after the
wind" (1:17).

Until he has convinced us this is so,
Qoheleth cannot get us to sit still long
enough for this Wholly Other God to find
us.

CHAPTER THREE

Happy Work

I thought in my heart, "Come now, I will test you with pleasure to find out what is good." But that also proved to be meaningless. "Laughter," I said, "is foolish. And what does pleasure accomplish?" I tried cheering myself with wine, and embracing folly—my mind still guiding me with wisdom. I wanted to see what was worthwhile for men to do under heaven during the few days of their lives.

I undertook great projects: I built houses for myself and planted vineyards. I made gardens and parks and planted all kinds of fruit trees in them. I made reservoirs to water groves of flourishing trees. I bought male and female slaves and had other slaves who were born in my house. I also owned more herds and flocks than anyone in Jerusalem before me. I amassed silver and gold for myself, and the treasure of kings and provinces. I acquired men and women singers, and a harem as well—the delights of the heart of man. I became greater by far than anyone in Jerusalem before me. In all this my wisdom stayed with me.

I denied myself nothing my eyes desired;
  I refused my heart no pleasure.
My heart took delight in all my work,

and this was the reward for all
  my labor.
Yet when I surveyed all that my
  hands had done
and what I had toiled to achieve,
everything was meaningless, a chasing
  after the wind;
nothing was gained under the sun.

Then I turned my thoughts to consider
  wisdom,
  and also madness and folly.
What more can the king's successor do
  than what has already been done?
I saw that wisdom is better than folly,
  just as light is better than darkness.
The wise man has eyes in his head,
  while the fool walks in the darkness;
but I came to realize
  that the same fate overtakes them
  both.

Then I thought in my heart,

"The fate of the fool will overtake me
  also.
  What then do I gain by being wise?"
I said in my heart,
  "This too is meaningless."
For the wise man, like the fool, will not
  be long remembered;

*in days to come both will be forgotten.
Like the fool, the wise man too must die!*

*So I hated life, because the work that
is done under the sun was grievous to me.
All of it is meaningless, a chasing after
the wind. I hated all the things I had
toiled for under the sun, because I must
leave them to the one who comes after
me. And who knows whether he will be a
wise man or a fool? Yet he will have control over all the work into which I have
poured my effort and skill under the sun.
This too is meaningless. So my heart
began to despair over all my toilsome
labor under the sun. For a man may do
his work with wisdom, knowledge and
skill, and then he must leave all he owns
to someone who has not worked for it.
This too is meaningless and a great misfortune. What does a man get for all the
toil and anxious striving with which he
labors under the sun? All his days his
work is pain and grief; even at night his
mind does not rest. This too is meaningless.*

*A man can do nothing better than to
eat and drink and find satisfaction in his
work. This too, I see, is from the hand of
God, for without him, who can eat or find
enjoyment? To the man who pleases him,
God gives wisdom, knowledge and happiness, but to the sinner he gives the task of
gathering and storing up wealth to hand
it over to the one who pleases God. This
too is meaningless, a chasing after the
wind.*

—*Ecclesiastes 2:1-26*

The problem with children and back-
yards in not that children sit idly in some
corner twiddling their thumbs, bored silly
because they cannot find anything to do.
On the contrary, they storm out there
with all sorts of grandiose plans they
make up along the way. They're pirates
chasing each other around and over the
picnic table. They get distracted by a
squirrel and try to climb up the tree after
it. When they tire of chasing this monster
up Mt. Everest, they look around for the
linoleum to build another fort.

The problem sets in when they don't
like what they have made themselves.
They become inconsolably frustrated.
The fort doesn't work out to their satisfaction, so it's "dumb." No amount of
adult praise or reason can change their
minds because no one can erase the pain
of their inability to build a decent fort.

No one except Grandpa. When they
notice him making faces at them again
from the upstairs window, they laugh.
They forget their failure and happily
return to their play.

Three Thought Experiments

Stephen Hawking is widely acclaimed
to be the most brilliant theoretical physi-
cist since Einstein. Incredibly, Hawking
cannot handle a telescope, operate
research equipment, or even speak. He
suffers from a progressive degenerative
disease that has left him permanently in a
wheelchair with only one means of com-
munication with the outside world: his
computer. Despite these incredible
deficits, Hawking steadily pushes our
knowledge of the cosmos into the twenty-
first century.

How? Since he cannot do physical
experiments, Hawking conducts thought
experiments in his head. Having mastered
the principles of physics as they function
in the real world, he embarks on journeys
of discovery in his own mind. An associate of Hawking's, John Boslough, writes:

Most days at work Hawking just
thinks. He spends much of his time

developing new approaches to problems in theoretical physics. One of his
colleagues, Ian Moss, told me one
morning, "Stephen comes up with all
the ideas. The rest of us only test them
out to see if they work."
—Stephen Hawking's Universe,
p. 19

With his incredible ability to retain
and manipulate pages of complex equa-
tions in his head, he creates one theoretical universe after another, discarding
those that break the known laws of
physics and using the remaining ones to
construct a working model of the universe as it may actually exist. He begins
his experiments with a hypothesis, a
"What if . . .," and chases it down to see
where it might lead in helping us to
understand the rules that keep reality
together. Often what he discovers in his
head turns out to explain a great deal of
what really happens "out there."

Qoheleth conducts similar thought
experiments to pursue his own chosen
field of interest: "to see what was worthwhile for men to do under heaven during
the few days of their lives" (2:3). He
assumes the identity of King Solomon,
the grandest, most successful, and wisest
king that God's people had ever known.
If anyone would have been able to
achieve lasting meaning in this world, it
was he. So Qoheleth conducts three
experiments based on that premise
(2:1-23): "What if I had as much fun as
Solomon? (2:1-11); What if I had his
wisdom? (2:12-16); What if I had his
property? (2:17-23) Would these things
make me achieve something meaningful
and lasting?"

Unlike Hawking's experiments,
Qoheleth's come up dry. And their failure
drives Qoheleth to find a higher truth,
one with which he concludes this chapter.

Round One: Pleasure Vaporizes (2:1-11)

The pursuit of pleasure launches
Qoheleth's first thought experiment:

*I thought in my heart, "Come now, I will
test you with pleasure to find out what is
good."*
(2:1)

The Hebrew word for "pleasure" cov-
ers a broad range of meanings: "joy,"
"gladness," "happiness." Unlike the
Greek philosophers, God's people of old
allowed no dichotomy between the joys
of this world and spiritual bliss. They
believed that all good things, material
and immaterial, that brought joy and happiness, should be valued as blessed gifts
from God himself. There is no better way
to celebrate the Sabbath, one rabbi
taught, than to spend half of it worshiping
God and the other half of it eating.
(History notes that this portly rabbi might
have done his waistline—if not his
soul—greater good by either revising that
ratio God-ward or finding some alternative ways of enjoying Saturdays!)

Carefully utilizing his great wisdom to
achieve and maximize his joy,
"Solomon"/Qoheleth works hard to create his very own little heaven on earth—
complete with wine, palaces, gardens (literally: "paradises") and women (*lots* of
women, 2:8 adds). What he describes
picks up much of what is actually report-
ed of Solomon in 1 Kings 4-11.

For a while it seemed to work:

*I denied myself nothing my eyes desired;
I refused my heart no pleasure. My heart*

took delight in all my work, and this was
the reward for all my labor.

(2:10)

Unlike so many who never even get to
first base, "Solomon"/Qoheleth gets to
enjoy the fruits of his hard work. But
when he takes a second look, he discovers that it's all meaningless—a breath, a
pretty bubble that bursts apart in no time
flat. "'Laughter,' I said, 'is foolish. And
what does pleasure accomplish?'" (2:2).
It's all just "a chasing after the wind;
nothing was gained under the sun"
(2:11). The bottom line remains where it
always was: at zero.

Looking for kicks at parties, at singles
bars, or in the bottom of a bottle gets to
be a relentlessly boring and tedious business. It provides some thrills for a while,
but every time you "score," you need a
bigger and better thrill. The cycle never
quits. Every desire filled creates only a
temporary buzz that vaporizes into a
yearning for an even better one. Sooner
or later that yearning can no longer be
sated, because, as Qoheleth already point-
ed out, "The eye never has enough of seeing, nor the ear its fill of hearing" (1:8).
That's why making happiness or fun the
aim of our lives turns out so empty,
pointless, and futile. Happiness only
endures if we live for something or someone who sticks around to keep making us
happy. Does Someone like that exist?

Round Two: Wisdom Vaporizes (2:12-16)

When Qoheleth finds that even
Solomonic success in the pursuit of plea-
sure would not make him lastingly
happy, he tests a second hypothesis.
Maybe the unmatched *wisdom* of
Solomon (2:12b) would let him achieve it.

As with his pursuit of pleasure, he
finds the initial results fairly encouraging:
"I saw that wisdom is better than folly,
just as light is better than darkness"
(2:13).

There, that's at least something. One
thing has more lasting value than another.
Maybe his teachers were right: the pursuit of wisdom might lead to something
he can hang onto. He remembers what
they taught him: "The wise man has eyes
in his head, while the fool walks in darkness (2:14)." At least traditional wisdom
and his own observations dovetail on this
point.

But his triumph does not last long.
When he thinks it through, he realizes
that he must look beyond these limited
observations. Yes, indeed, as long as they
live, the wise have the same kind of
advantage over fools as the sighted have
over the blind. But he observes something else too:

The same fate overtakes them both. Then
I thought in my heart, "The fate of the
fool will overtake me also. What then do I
gain by being wise?" I said in my heart,
"This too is meaningless." For the wise
man, like the fool, will not be long
remembered; in days to come both will
be forgotten. Like the fool, the wise man
too must die!

(2:14-16)

Death, the great equalizer of rich and
poor, happy and unhappy, wise and foolish, wipes out any limited advantage that
either joy or wisdom can bring. Whatever
profit the subtotal shows, death rolls back
to that same exasperating zero. Despite
its promising start, experiment two also
comes up dry.

Round Three: Possessions Vaporize (2:17-23)

A bank and a church bounded opposite sides of a cemetery. Since both tried to sell security in exchange for hard currency, they found themselves in direct competition for the consumer's purse strings. So they advertised. The bank put up a big sign: "You can't take it with you, but you can lie next to it." The church put up an even bigger sign: "You can't take it with you, but you can send it on ahead."

If the story were true, we'd undoubtedly have grounds for legal action. Contrary to the bank's claim, we cannot lie next to our wealth. The Egyptians tried that, hoping that by burying their possessions with them they could somehow hang onto them. But they found that a mummy and his money were soon parted.

The church sign lied too. We cannot send our money on ahead. First of all, whatever the currency we use in the New Jerusalem may turn out to be (if we still need any), it will certainly not be U.S. or Canadian dollars. Second, the only instruments of any value forwarded there for us will not be the monies or goods we have donated ourselves, but rather the complete and perfect works done by Jesus Christ on our behalf. He fulfilled all righteousness for us. Our account in heaven is already filled. We don't need to send any more on ahead. If we give to the church or to the needy, we do it only because the cause itself speaks to our hearts—not so that we can selfishly buy for ourselves bigger mansions in the sky.

Qoheleth points us in this direction by sharing with us the results of his third thought experiment: "What if I had the wealth of Solomon? Would that give me some sense of lasting meaning and accomplishment?"

His simple answer: No. We can heap up possession upon possession, but we cannot take our wealth with us. In fact, we cannot even leave it behind intact:

I hated all the things I had toiled for under the sun, because I must leave them to the one who comes after me. And who knows whether he will be a wise man or a fool? Yet he will have control over all the work into which I have poured my effort and skill under the sun. This too is meaningless.

(2:18-19)

Whatever wealth we accumulate will go to those who did not work for it. And sooner or later they will "fritter it all away" and there will be nothing left of it. As surely as the *nouveau riche* lose their wealth with a bang in their own lifetime, so "old money" hemorrhages into oblivion over the generations. In either case wealth vaporizes like everything else we try to achieve.

Qoheleth exposes the empty-headed, foolish materialism of capitalist and communist alike. He rejects the capitalist lie that hanging onto money really has any lasting merit: sooner or later we or our heirs will make it disappear. He also exposes the communist lie of a workers' paradise that we can build for our children and grandchildren. Such a paradise on earth will simply not materialize. There will always be more than enough fools in any generation to guarantee that the hoped-for "good life" will never appear. Communal as well as individual wealth will vaporize, negating all the sweat and tears and sacrifices poured into its accumulation.

But the problem with wealth goes deeper. The grief it causes does not begin only after death. Its icy grip already reaches us on this side of the grave:

What does a man get for all the toil and anxious striving with which he labors under the sun? All his days his work is pain and grief; even at night his mind does not rest. This too is meaningless.

(2:22-23)

How quickly our possessions begin to possess us! Do they serve us, or do we run around serving them? How much happiness, free time, and enjoyment of our relationships do we sacrifice to the god *Mammon* ? We work our fingers to the bone in order to pay off the mortgage, only to find out that when we actually own the house, our kids have already moved out of it. Where were we when they were growing up? Holding down two jobs and a paper route. Inevitably the day comes when we have to sell the place anyway and move into some kind of senior citizens' complex. Will the kids want to come and visit? Why would they?

When he discovers that even this third effort at finding lasting meaning in life fails him, Qoheleth falls into deep despair:

So I hated life, because the work that is done under the sun was grievous to me. All of it is meaningless, a chasing after the wind. I hated all the things I had toiled for under the sun.

(2:17)

But his hatred of life does not drive him to suicide—precisely because it is death that he fears most of all. More than anything else, that God-ordained bound-

ary to our existence makes our lives meaningless: God makes us a limited-time offer only. Then he tears it back out of our compulsively clenched hands.

Happy to Work (2:24-26)

Once he's taken his third strike and exited the batters' box, Qoheleth suddenly makes the overwhelmingly simple but crucial discovery that he's not there for the game; the game's there for him! He does not have to work to be happy; he can be happy just to work.

This sudden discovery makes Qoheleth shift directly from reverse into overdrive, from the frustrated lament of 2:23 to the confident, trusting confession that immediately follows:

There is no more good for a man than to eat and drink and find the good life in his work. This too, I saw, is from the hand of God; for apart from him, who can eat or find enjoyment? For to the man with good before his face, God gives wisdom, knowledge and joy, but to the sinner he gives the work of gathering and storing up to hand it over to the one who is good before God's face. This [gathering and storing by the sinner] too is meaningless, a chasing after the wind.

(2:24-26—author's translation)

Children know that Grandpa wants them to go and *do* something. But they forget that Grandpa tells them that because he wants them to enjoy themselves and *not* because he needs them to accomplish great things for him. So they become frustrated, and they turn the backyard into a pressure cooker. Worst of all, their compulsive, strenuous efforts make them lose sight of Grandpa himself, and they feel increasingly forlorn and abandoned. They don't even remember to

look up at the window anymore. This is
hardly what Grandpa had in mind.

His investigation has convinced
Qoheleth that we can accomplish nothing
meaningful and lasting "under the sun."
But we don't have to! He looks up
beyond the sun to the One who is in
heaven, whose works last forever. It is
God and God alone who gives us daily
bread, joy, and meaning in life. God
freely gives us what we cannot achieve
for ourselves. How sad when, instead of
gratefully enjoying what he gives us, we
squander God's gifts by trying to construct our own salvation. Out of sheer
grace, through the gift of his son, God
hands us the kingdom of heaven on a silver platter. But we neglect it because
we're so busy building our own.

This is the burden of Qoheleth: to
show us how wasteful we are of God's
free and bountiful grace when we try to
find lasting meaning in our own efforts
instead of in our relationship to him.
Having taken us to the fence and back,
wise Qoheleth redirects our attention to
the upstairs window so that our work can
once more be joy-filled play with no
other purpose than to make our neighbor,
ourselves, and our God really happy.
"Look, Grandpa, LOOK! See what *I* can
do!"

CHAPTER FOUR

Spinning Wheel

There is a time for everything,
and a season for every activity
under heaven:
a time to be born and a time to die,
a time to plant and a time to uproot,
a time to kill and a time to heal,
a time to tear down and a time to build,
a time to weep and a time to laugh,
a time to mourn and a time to dance,
a time to scatter stones and a time to
*   gather them,*
a time to embrace and a time to refrain,
a time to search and a time to give up,
a time to keep and a time to throw away,
a time to tear and a time to mend,
a time to be silent and a time to speak,
a time to love and a time to hate,
a time for war and a time for peace.

What does the worker gain from his
toil? I have seen the burden God has laid
on men. He has made everything beauti-
ful in its time. He has also set eternity in
the hearts of men; yet they cannot fathom
what God has done from beginning to
end. I know that there is nothing better
for men than to be happy and do good
while they live. That everyone may eat
and drink, and find satisfaction in all his
toil—this is the gift of God. I know that
everything God does will endure forever;

nothing can be added to it and
nothing taken from it. God does
it so that men will revere him.

Whatever is has already been,
*   and what will be has been before;*
*   and God will call the past to account.*
*   —Ecclesiastes 3:1-15*

When we are young, we want to be
older. A toddler wants to be as old as his
big sister so he too can ride a bike and go
on the school bus. As a teeny-bopper, he
can't wait for that most resplendent of all
days: the day that a driver's license finally graces his wallet. Barely into senior
high, he already longs for graduation so
he can head for college or bring home
that first paycheck. As a young adult, he
dreams of finding the right girl and set-
tling down, and soon after the wedding,
of buying a house and raising a family.
Locked into a mortgage, tuition pay-
ments, and a job that never gets any easi-
er, he begins increasingly to look forward
to retirement. And when he's finally
reached his "golden years," he hungers to
be young again. . . .

On Schedule (3:1, 9)

We can guess by now what wise Qoheleth would say about that restless striving, and he does not disappoint us. With wisdom's call to live by grace, not by works, still ringing in his head, he seeks to apply it to the question mark posed by the wheel of time. The endless cycles of generations coming and going, of harvest time following sowing time, of peace following war following peace— what do these relentlessly reoccurring cycles mean? In verses 2 through 8 he lists fourteen examples, framing them, as he did his introductory poem (1:3-11), with this very practical concern: what is their impact on us working stiffs?

For everything there is a season, and a time for every matter under heaven.
(3:1 RSV)

What does the worker gain from his toil?
(3:9)

The Hebrew language in Qoheleth's day had no way of expressing the abstract concept of time. So Qoheleth uses words that refer only to concrete, specific moments of our everyday existence. The word for "time" that he uses continuously in verses 2 through 8 carries with it the idea of something happening at just the appropriate time, such as turning in a term paper just before the deadline, or finding the pension check in the mail the day before the rent is due.

A Time for This and That (3:2-8)

In verses 2 through 8 Qoheleth lists fourteen pairs of opposites, each separated simply by the word "and." There may be some significance in the fact that he chose to include exactly a multiple of seven. Perhaps he intended to echo the seven creation days and point to the completeness or fullness of the cycles. Maybe he even wanted to hint at their divine origin. Hebraic authors often used such literary devices, and that may be the case here too.

Commentators have found no obvious pattern or structure to the way Qoheleth has placed these cycles in the list. They do point out that he begins with the cycle that offers the greatest extremes (at least to us mortals): "a time to be born and a time to die" (3:2).

Each couplet lists opposites: "born/die"; "plant/uproot"; "kill/heal"; and so on. By stating the opposing limits, Qoheleth, in typical Hebrew fashion, wants to include everything in between as well. Between birth and death we experience lots of other regularly recurring cycles: bath times and supper times, vacation times and overtimes. Between planting and uprooting there are also lots of recurring activities: watering, pruning, and picking. So without trying to be exhaustive in identifying the cycles of life, he does strive to be comprehensive.

The list deals with generalities. We should respect that and not try to nail down specifically what the Teacher meant by, for example, "a time to kill." Kill what or whom? For what purpose? Qoheleth does not tell us. His thesis that there is an appropriate time for everything refers to animal sacrifice as well as to taking life on the battlefield. The scattering of stones could refer to renovating an old house as well as to ruining an enemy's field. He purposely leaves his examples unmodified, wide open to the broadest possible range of applications.

On the basis of this list Qoheleth points us once again to that sobering bottom line: "What profit has the toiler from

his toil?" (3:9—author's translation).
Scanning this ongoing cycle of
birth/death, rooting/uprooting,
killing/healing, loving/hating, we cannot
deny that all our hard efforts basically
don't change anything. The wheel just
keeps on grinding and, try as we might,
we cannot prevent ourselves from being
spun along, locked inextricably into its
gears. Our lifelong efforts to hang on to
this or that will fail. So will our attempts
at getting rid of something once and for
all. What comes goes. What goes comes.
Nothing we do can change that.

God-Spun (3:15)

Once again Qoheleth observes that the
ever-turning cycles of our lives do not
just happen; they are spun by God:

That which is, already has been; that
which is to be, already has been; and
God seeks what has been driven away.
(3:15 RSV)

Some commentators assume that the
Teacher's pessimism forces him to discard the biblical notion of time as linear,
as a historical process that God takes
from one place (i.e., bondage in Egypt) to
a very different one, from which we shall
never return (i.e., the promised land for
Israel; the New Jerusalem for us). They
argue that Qoheleth has lost all hope of
God continuing redemptive history and
leading his people to a better world. They
contend that instead, by listing the cycles
of life, he has opted for the pagan notion
of time as an ever-spinning wheel that
will never stop revolving, but will always
leave us hopelessly stuck. In their view,
Qoheleth concludes that the wheels of
God's derailed salvation train spin help-
lessly in the mire without any chance of
ever getting anywhere again.

That, however, is clearly not the case.
Nowhere does Qoheleth argue this way.
Rather he teaches that our own efforts,
our own struggling under the sun, our
own attempts to think our way out cause
this frustration of not getting anywhere.
Consistently this makes Qoheleth look
beyond the sun to heaven. He specifically
reminds us time and again that God can
and will come through for us. However,
within that historical process that continues from creation through the fall and
through God's work of recreation to
Judgment Day (cf. 12:14!), the recurring
patterns are not only discernable, but
stand out clearly and visibly. Certainly
we're cycling on the road to somewhere.
But on our trip the wheels just go round
and round, mile after mile, year after
year.

Someday God will radically alter the
entire universe and our own existence
(for the better). But we live in the present. And our present is governed by
times and seasons that come and go
under God's supervision. Those cycles
began eons before we were born and may
continue for a long time after we're gone.
How are we to live wisely in the meantime? This is Qoheleth's concern.

God-Given Busyness (3:10-11)

Qoheleth derives three important conclusions from watching God spin the
world round and round. The first:

I have seen the business that God has
given to the sons of men to be busy with.
He has made everything beautiful in its
time.
(3:10-11a RSV)

The Teacher observes that the wheel
of life is not in itself vicious. In fact, all
the things that occur and reoccur are

beautiful *in their God-appointed time*. It is appropriate and right and seemly for children to behave like children. But that same behavior becomes ugly and unacceptable when it comes from an adult. The joys of sexual union, so wonderful and enriching in a fully committed, mature marriage relationship, are selfish and dirty when couples get too far ahead of themselves physically. Like eating a peach before it's ripe, it spoils and sours what, given enough time, would blossom into a delightful God-given gift. That's why the Song of Songs keeps sounding its wise refrain to young lovers: "Do not arouse or awaken love until it so desires" (Song of Songs 2:7).

In the same vein, a comment made at the right time can do a world of good. But spoken out of turn it cripples.

What makes the circles ugly are our human attempts either to slow them down or to accelerate them. Like a child throwing a tantrum at bedtime, we often rebel against what God has ordained: "I know that everything that God does will endure forever; nothing can be added to it and nothing taken from it" (3:14).

Enjoy the roses while they bloom, and when they're gone, enjoy the crisp October air and then the velvet winter snow instead. Enjoy being a kid, and when you're older, enjoy the kids while you still have them. And when advancing time leaves you without youth and youths, then enjoy the peace and quiet.

A Tantalizing Peek (3:11, 14)

The ancient Greeks tell the story of poor King Tantalus, who, like poor Sisyphus, ran afoul of the gods. For his crime he was placed beside a beautiful, cool, crystal-clear pond on a scorching summer day. Overcome by thirst, Tantalus stooped down to drink, but as he bent down, the water level also dropped, and he could not reach it. So he fell to his knees. But the water stayed out of reach. Whenever he stood, the level would rise, and the refreshing water would beckon. But at each desperate effort, it would teasingly drop just beyond his reach.

Qoheleth's second conclusion contends that God similarly tantalizes us:

[God] has also set eternity in the hearts of men; yet they cannot fathom what God has done from beginning to end.

(3:11b)

God has given us a taste of eternity. Unlike the animals who live only for the day, we are able to look back at the past, and we can gaze into the future. We have the ability to "pop" out of our own skin and examine our lives against the backdrop of massive quantities of time in both directions. But God gives us this ability in such a limited way that, like Tantalus, it leaves us thirsty and frustrated. It fails to satisfy the eager longing for complete understanding that this view of eternity creates within us. Powerful as it is, it does not let us understand what God is up to. We catch a glimpse of the puzzle, but not enough to get the picture, and certainly not enough to know where the bits and pieces of our own lives fit into it. God gives us no road map of the past or the future by which we can chart our own course in the present. He gives us no way of controlling, or even influencing, our own destiny.

Why does God give us this ability to experience eternity in our thoughts but not the chance to derive any understanding or lasting meaning from it? Why should we constantly bump into this additional limit that God has set for us?

Unlike the gods who took revenge on poor Tantalus, God has no stomach for teasing or torturing us. Instead "God does it so that men will revere him" (3:14).

If we failed to realize our total dependence on God, we might all too easily ignore God and scoff at the idea of walking in his ways. Traditional Hebrew wisdom expressed a similar fear:

Give me neither poverty nor riches, but give me only my daily bread. Otherwise, I may have too much and disown you and say, "Who is the LORD?"
—Proverbs 30:8-9

The wheel of life goes round and round for a good reason, claims Qoheleth. Although we cannot figure out how, it continually spins the fabric of our relationship to God. We need to know that. Instead of constantly rebelling against what he has ordained, we must learn to live every day out of God's hand, accepting and making the most of what he sees fit to give us in *his* own good time. *He* is God. And we are God's creatures who owe our Creator proper awe, respect, and obedience (this idea in the Hebrew literally means "fear").

That's a far cry from the kind of rebellion that taunts God to drag us along kicking and screaming. It's also far removed from a defeated fatalism that makes us simply go limp, stoically allowing God to cart us off like passive resisters at a protest rally. God is not some pigheaded dictator. He is the one, true, loving God who seeks to shower us with grace. Therefore God has every right to expect our willing assent and eager compliance. God deserves our active response and our full trust that whatever he gives us is indeed good (*tov*) for this

moment of our lives—even if we cannot begin to imagine how.

By obediently walking at God's pace, neither standing still nor seeking to outdistance him, we can relate to our Maker as we should, in all humility and sincerity. We do not know the whole picture. Hand in hand with our Dad (*Abba*, Rom. 8:15) we do not need to know. He is God. He knows the way.

Our Greatest Good (3:12-13)

This leads Qoheleth to his third conclusion, one that sounds again his favorite refrain:

I realized there is no greater good in them than to be happy and do good while they live; and also everyone who eats and drinks and sees good in all his toil—that is God's gift to them.
(3:12-13—author's translation)

As he did in 2:24-26, Qoheleth places a heavy emphasis on the word *good* (*tov* in each instance). With it he answers his own fundamental inquiry into "what was worthwhile [good] (Hebrew: *tov*) for people to do under heaven during the few days of their lives" (2:3). He answers: this is good, to enjoy the good that God gives you and to allow God's goodness to come through in everything you do, even your work. In every season of your life, whether difficult or easy, be sure to treasure and utilize the unique gifts God gives you.

The youngsters in Grandpa's backyard cannot stay out there forever. They need to come in for supper. They have to take a bath and hop into the sack on time. Of course, being children, they prefer to set their own schedules. But Grandpa is not mean enough to let them do that. They cannot understand why they have to

come inside *now*, while they're having
such a good time. But when they stop
fussing and do what Grandpa says,
they're happiest—in the long run.

CHAPTER FIVE

A Handful of Nothing

*And I saw something else under
     the sun:
In the place of judgment—
     wickedness was there,
     in the place of justice—wickedness
     was there.*

I thought in my heart,

*"God will bring to judgment
     both the righteous and the wicked,
for there will be a time for every activity,
     a time for every deed."*

*I also thought, "As for men, God tests
them so that they may see that they are
like the animals. Man's fate is like that of
the animals; the same fate awaits them
both: As one dies, so dies the other. All
have the same breath; man has no advantage over the animal. Everything is meaningless. All go to the same place; all
come from dust, and to dust all return.
Who knows if the spirit of man rises
upward and if the spirit of the animal
goes down into the earth?"*

*So I saw that there is nothing better
for a man than to enjoy his work, because
that is his lot. For who can bring him to
see what will happen after him?*

*Again I looked and saw all
     the oppression that was taking
     place under the sun:*

*I saw the tears of the oppressed—
     and they have no comforter;
power was on the side of their oppres
     sors—
     and they have no comforter.
And I declared that the dead,
     who had already died,
are happier than the living,
     who are still alive.
But better than both is he
     who has not yet been,
who has not seen the evil
     that is done under the sun.*

*And I saw that all labor and all
achievement spring from man's envy of
his neighbor. This too is meaningless, a
chasing after the wind.*

*The fool folds his hands
     and ruins himself.
Better one handful with tranquillity
     than two handfuls with toil
     and chasing after the wind.*

*Again I saw something meaningless
under the sun:*

39

There was a man all alone;
  he had neither son nor brother.
There was no end to his toil,
  yet his eyes were not content with his
    wealth.
"For whom am I toiling," he asked,
  "and why am I depriving myself of
    enjoyment?"
This too is meaningless—
  a miserable business!

Two are better than one,
  because they have a good return for
    their work:
If one falls down,
  his friend can help him up.
But pity the man who falls
  and has no one to help him up!
Also, if two lie down together, they will
    keep warm.
  But how can one keep warm alone?
Though one may be overpowered,
  two can defend themselves.
A cord of three strands is not quickly bro-
    ken.

Better a poor but wise youth than an
old but foolish king who no longer knows
how to take warning. The youth may have
come from prison to the kingship, or he
may have been born in poverty within his
kingdom. I saw that all who lived and
walked under the sun followed the youth,
the king's successor. There was no end to
all the people who were before them. But
those who came later were not pleased
with the successor. This too is meaning-
less, a chasing after the wind.
                —Ecclesiastes 3:16-4:16

In Chapter 1 Qoheleth began by stating his major problem: all that we do under the sun is meaningless. Then in Chapter 2 he took us on three thought experiments that led him to his conclusion that our only meaning lies in our relationship to God (2:24-26). In Chapter 3 he showed us how the cycles of life make sense only when we take the time to accept and enjoy them as God gives them to us. Now, in the last part of Chapter 3 and through Chapter 4, he applies this wisdom to five further examples of meaninglessness that he bumps into in his exploratory forays under the sun: abasement, advantage, achievement, aloneness, and advancement.

Abasement: A Struggle with Injustice (3:16-22)

In this brief section we see a typical example of Qoheleth's way of working through a problem: an observation (3:16) evokes a traditional response (3:17); but further observation shows that response to be incomplete (3:18-21) and therefore leads the Teacher to form his own conclusion (3:22).

Qoheleth begins with the observation that in this world we would expect to find justice, because God ordains whatever goes on down here. But instead of justice we find wickedness! How does that square with the notion of a righteous God?

His knee-jerk response is to immediately reach back to the traditional answer his own teachers had given him:

God will bring to judgment both the
righteous and the wicked, for there will
be a time for every activity, a time for
every deed.
                                    (3:17)

"Hold on now, young fella," we can almost hear the traditional teachers say. "Slow down now! In his own good time God will square all accounts. Be patient, sit through a few more scenes, and sooner or later the story will end as it should with the bad guys in the slammer and the good guys living happily ever after."

But upon reflection, Qoheleth is not really satisfied with that answer. Qoheleth observes that if God is going to square up accounts, he'd better hurry up. Before long both the righteous and the wicked will bite the dust (3:20). Then any such accounting—divine or otherwise—will make no further difference, since death will wipe out any lasting distinction between the good and the evil.

We're presently raising the third generation of TV consumers on a steady diet of cop shows and sitcoms. These shows proclaim that goodness and right triumph in the end and that crime doesn't really pay. We badly need to hear the Teacher's Spirit-guided message. If we're putting our hopes here under the sun on some tidy scheme in which God always lets good succeed and evil fail, then we're in for a rude shock. It's just not happening. Don't bet the family minivan on the premise that living justly will pay off handsomely. Like all our other deeds, if our own morality and decency and uprightness have become goals in and of themselves, then we're chasing the wind. Justice detached from our relationship to God has no lasting value.

To save us from putting all our eggs in the basket of our own overblown righteousness, Qoheleth reminds us that "God tests [people] so that they may see that they are like the animals" (3:18).

Qoheleth doesn't wish to enter the creation/science controversy here. He has no interest in theorizing about our ancestry. He only wants to point out that humans and animals are alike in this way at least:

The same fate awaits them both: As one dies, so dies the other. All have the same breath; man has no advantage over the animal. Everything is meaningless.

(3:19)

Qoheleth reminds us that here, too, we bump into that familiar fence beyond which we cannot see: death. Just as we cannot take our money with us, so we cannot take our good deeds or our sense of fair play along. Death will level out all differences between the just and the unjust. Even if, during this life, God lets everything subtotal properly by making the righteous better off, death still ultimately brings the bottom line back down to nil for both! And after we die, will all our present striving for justice make any difference? Who knows?

Who knows if the spirit of man rises upward and if the spirit of the animal goes down into the earth?

(3:21)

Respect the limit God has set to your knowledge, Qoheleth advises. Forget your highbrow speculations on the differences between good guys and bad guys, humans and beasts. Just see

that there is nothing better for a man than to enjoy his work, because that is his lot. For who can bring him to see what will happen after him?

(3:22)

How God will square accounts we do not and cannot know.

How, or even *if*, our own righteousness will give us any big advantage is also not clear. All we know is that God has given us good stuff to do (Hebrew:

tov), and we may enjoy doing it *for its own sake*. And that's *good* enough! Does our New Testament understanding of the resurrection from the dead make this Old Testament teacher's conclusion obsolete? Hardly.

Let's admit that we still know precious little about what life will be like on the other side of the vale. Jesus, Paul, and John have given us a few titillating peeks. But how will our lives lived here actually impact our lives on the other side? All we know is that over there we'll fully benefit from Christ's righteousness, not our own. So if we live justly down here, we should not be doing so in the hope of ferrying our bag of "goodies" over the Jordan.

Rather, our righteousness itself is a good gift from God to us—a gift we may enjoy; a gift we may share; a gift we may cultivate in ourselves, our church, our nation, and our world. But since Jesus has fulfilled all righteousness for us, we need not lose any sleep over the injustices still remaining in this "vale of tears." All we need to understand is that, in his own good time, God has already begun to tackle this ugly mystery of injustice in ourselves and in the world by letting us nail it to a cross on Golgotha.

Nobody has been more patient in suffering the most cruel injustices of all than God has. God saw his beloved child tortured and murdered before his eyes. How freely he has turned our limited, human (self-)righteousness on its head to show us justice that's literally out of this world. That massive transfusion of heaven-sent blood makes doing justice something we can't just talk about. It makes justice our own lifeblood. Never mind what lasting good it does, and never mind what consequences it might have trans-Jordan: our God-given new life makes us find no greater enjoyment than to splash around daily in that ocean of Spirit-poured righteousness.

Advantage and Achievement: Hollow Victories (4:1-6)

"THEY CALL THIS LIVING?" It's scary how at a distance of more than two thousand years and half a world away Qoheleth could so naturally join with us in that familiar office-bound, car-pool lament. Why do we do it—this endless rat race? Where do all our efforts to claw and bite and gouge our way to the top get us except sleepless nights and a belly full of ulcers? Why can't we give it a rest?

Qoheleth's answer: "I saw that all labor and all achievement spring from a man's envy of his neighbor. This too is meaningless, a chasing after the wind" (4:4).

We want to keep up with the Joneses. So we work like slaves, and we don't mind if we get what we want by stepping on the backs of the poor and the needy. So what if the greatest killer of children in the Third World is measles—for lack of a lousy ten-cent vaccination? So kids in the barrios of Mexico City are literally rotting their brains out of their heads because they never get enough protein in their diet to feed a stinking rat. What does that have to do with us? "They have no comforter" (4:1), but that silk-tied, smooth-talking Jones has a better crack at the supervisor job than we do. So we spend our time working longer hours and kissing up to the boss. And Jones gets himself a four-head VCR and ours has only two. So we need a better one too. And we're so busy paying bills that we have neither the time, the money, nor the inclination to dry the tears from the faces of dirty, Third-World brats.

"Best never to have seen such evil," contends the Teacher. (4:2, 3) What a miserable, empty, meaningless business! The oppressed have no one to stick up for them because those who have more than enough make themselves much too busy trying to scramble ahead of everybody else.

Qoheleth can only offer some balanced advice: Don't make the mistake of giving up and cutting out of the rat race altogether. As his teachers warned: "The fool folds his hands and ruins himself" (4:5).

But this proverb's early foreshadowing of the Protestant work ethic only tells one side of the story:

Better one handful with tranquillity than two handfuls with toil and chasing after the wind.

(4:6)

The fool who rots in bed will go empty-handed. But those who constantly work their fingers to the bone won't be much better off. They'll have both hands full but will gain no satisfaction from it. They'll just get frustrated that their hands are not just a bit bigger so they can hold a little more (Luke 12:18). They're always working so hard that they never give themselves the chance to enjoy what they already have. That too is a meaningless business.

No, says Qoheleth, better to work for your basic needs and then learn to switch off that engine of greed. Learn to take the time not only to acquire but also to enjoy what you're acquiring. Enjoy some tranquillity. Buy some real peace by drying some Third-World tears. You'll have less cash, but you'll really enjoy what you have left.

Aloneness: The Misery of the Miser (4:7-12)

We've all heard stories of bums and bag ladies who live in abject squalor on skid row and who turn out to be multi-millionaires. We may even have met Howard Hughes types whose only thrill in life comes from watching the figures rise in their bank accounts. These misers work and worry, sweat and slave, denying themselves all other enjoyments because their addiction is not to the money itself, but to the buzz they get from watching it grow. That's why their eyes are never content with their wealth (4:8)— because one can always envision filling one more vertical column before the decimal. Worst of all, their enslavement to the figures on their investment portfolios causes them to deny themselves the most truly enriching thing of all, the warmth and happiness of meaningful human relationships.

What a miserable business, the Teacher observes. Here we find some of the few people in this world who really seem to be getting somewhere with their hard work, but they discover too late that it really isn't any fun exulting in the latest stock quotes when the only cocelebrants turn out to be empty chairs and blank walls. Having sold off any hope of finding somebody in life that matters, the miser cannot even look forward to the fleeting joy (see 2:18-19) of at least making a loved one happy with an inheritance after he's gone.

In applying his wisdom to the miser's plight, Qoheleth points out that denying oneself the joy of human relationships is not only dull and lonely, but it can actually be lethal. He gives three examples.

For solitary travelers in the rough Palestinian outback, one slip could spell a

disastrous fall. Such a fall could mean
hours or days of suffering a slow, painful
death with no hope of rescue. As prudent
swimmers and backwoods hikers do today,
travelers back then heeded, whenever possible, wisdom's call to "buddy up."

In our journey through life we all take
a tumble now and again. It's foolish to
imagine that we're so self-sufficient that
we never need help. Rugged individual-
ism can be an idol that not only robs us of
meaningful connections with others, but
steals our health, our well-being, and our
lives as well. In this example Qoheleth
clearly advocates neither independence,
nor a sickly, leeching dependency, but
*inter*dependence. Good friends who help
each other up when they're down "have a
good return for their work" (4:9): mutual
protection.

Qoheleth borrows a second example
from a long Palestinian journey: "If two
lie down together, they will keep warm.
But how can one keep warm alone?"
(4:11). With our abundance of travel
inns, campgrounds, and down-filled
sleeping bags, it may be difficult for us to
grasp the significance of some additional
body warmth on a cold night. But night-
time conditions in Qoheleth's setting
resembled more the harsh cold and isola-
tion of the high Arctic than the inviting
cheer of a summer evening marshmallow
roast in Yellowstone Park. Having someone to snuggle up to could make the vital
difference between surviving the night
and freezing to death.

Qoheleth's third example refers to a
common danger of the road posed by
lurking bandits who could easily overcome a hapless, solitary pilgrim, but who
would think twice about attacking a
group. In tandem, travelers could better
meet that threat.

Finally, Qoheleth attaches a proverb
that sums up the main point in each of
these three examples.

Though one may be overpowered, two
can defend themselves. A cord of three
strands is not quickly broken.

(4:12)

Using a typical Hebrew method of
building up the force of his argument by
counting upwards, Qoheleth emphasizes
the great advantage of communal effort.
If two can defend themselves, three can
do so even better—the more the merrier.
Here he sums up his whole approach to
the meaninglessness of abasement,
advantage, achievement, and aloneness.
He points out that healthy cooperation by
as many people as possible offers a wise
alternative to the rat race with its savage,
backbreaking competition in which even
the fittest survive only long enough to
find out that they are desperately alone,
unloved, and without identity.

Walter Wangerin, Jr., points out how
deeply God has rooted within us that
need for community. He writes:

> Listen: particular and loving relation-
> ships are more than merely "good";
> they are an essential quality of life.
> They affirm the individual's being.
> They assure him that he is. They both
> support him physically and define him
> spiritually. They give him a special
> place in the world, and they acknowl-
> edge the good purpose of his presence
> in that place. It is more than comfort
> we receive from other people: it is
> identity, so I know who I am. It is
> being itself, and the conviction of per-
> sonal worth.
> —As For Me And My House,
> *p. 58*

That is why the apostle Paul so urgently calls Christians to true community rooted in Christ. Such community does not merely round out the frilly edges of their lives, like a bridge club or a bowling league. It defines their very identity. In 1 Corinthians 12 and 13 Paul uses the new reality of Christ's work on earth to color in the vision of believers woven together so strongly in the love of Christ that they form Christ's perfectly functioning Body on earth.

But how easily Satan still employs the age-old strategy of divide-and-conquer! He cannot snap the three-strand cord (4:12). But he can break it strand by fraying strand: arguments over who should take out the garbage or do the dishes; battles over who may serve in church office or how old we think the earth is. And what gain is there for any Christ-follower in that? Like Barnabas and Paul, in our brokenness we may sometimes have to part company. But whenever we do, something in Christ's Body dies.

Advancement: A Fleeting Pleasure (4:13-16)

To make sure we do not imagine that sound relationships, important as they are, provide the ultimate answer to our quest for lasting meaning, Qoheleth quickly adds a fifth example to remind us of the inevitable limits to *any* human effort, including that of community building.

He cites the example of a poor but wise youth who snatched the throne away from its aging owner. Unlike this foolish incumbent, who should have been old enough to know better, this upstart knew the importance of teamwork. He listened to his advisors, and he played up to the crowds. He knew how important it was to get the community on his side. He became so successful at it that

all who lived and walked under the sun followed the youth, the king's successor. There was no end to all the people who were before them.

(4:15-16)

However, sad to say, "Those who came later were not pleased with the successor" (4:16). Just as capitalists must leave their legacy to those who will sooner or later squander it (3:18-19), communists will find their efforts to realize the workers' paradise fail because their faith in "the people" is equally unjustified. Public opinion is incredibly fickle. The will of the masses changes direction as arbitrarily and stupidly as a drunk in a maze. One day we ride the crest of public support and approval. The next we're unceremoniously dumped for a leader who moves in precisely the opposite direction.

What applies to the individual applies to the collective as well: all that we build up by our hard toil will ultimately fall apart. The wise work of this bright young "democrat" brought him a long way for a while, even further than the lonely miser who only acquired wealth. But his inevitable fall from (the people's) grace made his toil also evaporate in a puff of air. "This too is meaningless (Hebrew: "breath"), a chasing after wind" (4:16).

Christ calls members of his church to faithfully serve as community builders. And we're much better off actively belonging to the Body than sitting on the sidelines uselessly lonely in our efforts. But we may never forget that the New Jerusalem, the perfect society in which all will perfectly commune with God in Christ, comes not by our own efforts but

as a gift from heaven (Rev. 21:2). God
alone can do what is truly lasting. And he
will do it. Our own attempts at building
community will fail. Sooner or later the
roof will cave in on our buildings, our
congregations, our denominations, our
institutions, and our organizations. All
these earthly constructs must vanish to
make room for God's heavenly gift.

Since we live by grace through faith
and not by works, that fact should neither
startle nor disappoint us. Nor should it
make us stop seeking true community
here under the sun. Where our Lord
allows us to find it we enjoy it. And
through our happy fellowship we point
others also beyond our own failing efforts
to the mystery of the One who dwells
among us—who builds his church for
good.

CHAPTER SIX

The Sacrifice of Fools and Previous Matters

Guard your steps when you go to the house of God. Go near to listen rather than to offer the sacrifice of fools, who do not know that they do wrong.

Do not be quick with your mouth,
    do not be hasty in your heart
    to utter anything before God.
God is in heaven
    and you are on earth,
    so let your words be few.

As a dream comes when there are many
        cares,
    so the speech of a fool when there are
        many words.

When you make a vow to God, do not delay in fulfilling it. He has no pleasure in fools; fulfill your vow. It is better not to vow than to make a vow and not fulfill it. Do not let your mouth lead you into sin. And do not protest to the temple messenger, "My vow was a mistake." Why should God be angry at what you say and destroy the work of your hands? Much dreaming and many words are meaningless. Therefore stand in awe of God.

If you see the poor oppressed in a district, and justice and rights denied, do not be surprised at such things; *for one official is eyed by a higher one, and over them both are others higher still. The increase from the land is taken by all; the king himself profits from the fields.*

Whoever loves money never has money
        enough;
    whoever loves wealth is never satisfied
        with his income.
This too is meaningless.

As goods increase,
    so do those who consume them.
And what benefit are they to the owner
    except to feast his eyes on them?

The sleep of a laborer is sweet,
    whether he eats little or much,
but the abundance of a rich man
    permits him no sleep.

I have seen a grievous evil under the sun:
wealth hoarded to the harm of its owner,
    or wealth lost through some misfor-
        tune,
so that when he has a son
    there is nothing left for him.
Naked a man comes from his mother's
        womb,

and as he comes, so he departs.
He takes nothing from his labor
that he can carry in his hand.

This too is a grievous evil:

As a man comes, so he departs,
and what does he gain,
since he toils for the wind?

All his days he eats in darkness,
with great frustration, affliction and
anger.

Then I realized that it is good and
proper for a man to eat and drink, and to
find satisfaction in his toilsome labor
under the sun during the few days of life
God has given him—for this is his lot.
Moreover, when God gives any man
wealth and possessions, and enables him
to enjoy them, to accept his lot and be
happy in his work—this is a gift of God.
He seldom reflects on the days of his life,
because God keeps him occupied with
gladness of heart.

I have seen another evil under the sun,
and it weighs heavily on men: God gives
a man wealth, possessions and honor, so
that he lacks nothing his heart desires,
but God does not enable him to enjoy
them, and a stranger enjoys them instead.
This is meaningless, a grievous evil.

A man may have a hundred children
and live many years; yet no matter how
long he lives, if he cannot enjoy his pros-
perity and does not receive proper burial,
I say that a stillborn child is better off
than he. It comes without meaning, it
departs in darkness, and in darkness its
name is shrouded. Though it never saw
the sun or knew anything, it has more
rest than does that man—even if he lives
a thousand years twice over but fails to

enjoy his prosperity. Do not all go to the
same place?

All man's efforts are for his mouth,
yet his appetite is never satisfied.
What advantage has a wise man
over a fool?
What does a poor man gain
by knowing how to conduct himself
before others?
Better what the eye sees
than the roving of the appetite.
This too is meaningless,
a chasing after the wind.

Whatever exists has already been named,
and what man is has been known;
no man can contend
with one who is stronger than he.
The more the words,
the less the meaning,
and how does that profit anyone?

For who knows what is good for a
man in life, during the few and meaning-
less days he passes through like a shad-
ow? Who can tell him what will happen
under the sun after he is gone?
—Ecclesiastes 5 and 6

Before wandering back and reinvesti-
gating some of the ground he has covered
previously, Qoheleth adds one more
example to the list of human activities
that prove to be meaningless: the fleeting
"breath" (Hebrew: *hevel*) of worship that
amounts to nothing more than so much
"hot air."

Pious Blather (5:1-7)

Of all the things we do under the sun,
what could be more important than to
communicate directly with our God in
worship? Surely here, at the point of
meeting between weak, fallible mortals

and their all-powerful, eternal Creator there must be something very important, significant, and lasting going on.

The Teacher certainly does not deny it. But precisely because our meeting with God is so important, he gives us four cautions as we approach the throne of the Almighty.

Watch Out! (5:1-3)

In his first admonition Qoheleth warns:

Guard your steps when you go to the house of God. Go near to listen rather than to offer the sacrifice of fools, who do not know that they do wrong.

(5:1)

"Guard your feet," he warns. That's a Hebrew way of saying "watch your step." When we seek to communicate with God, we must come first of all to listen. The word in Hebrew means more than just "listen." It signifies willing obedience, similar to our word *heed*. We should heed what God has to say instead of "offer[ing] the sacrifice of fools" (5:1).

What he means by that curious turn of phrase becomes clear in his next word of warning:

Do not be quick with your mouth, do not be hasty in your heart to utter anything before God. God is in heaven and you are on the earth, so let your words be few.

(5:2)

God gave us two ears and only one mouth. We should take that to heart— especially when we appear before him. When it really hits home before whom we stand, speechless awe and reverence should characterize our worship rather than a flood of religious rhetoric.

Remember, Qoheleth reminds us, God is in heaven. What God does lasts forever. What God says really counts. But we are here on earth, below the sun. Our words have no more lasting value than our toil. Unlike the pagans, who imagine that without their sacrifices the gods would starve, we know only too well that the Almighty does not depend for survival on our puny efforts (Ps. 50:8-15). The shoe is always on the other foot.

Qoheleth does not want to rule out our joyful, grateful response to God's Word. Certainly that remains an important part of worship. He recognizes that God wants and enjoys our adoration and offerings, even though he does not need them.

But we must remain vigilant so that we do not drown out the Word of God with our own words.

Often in our conversations with others we do not really listen to them. We're much too busy thinking of what we want to tell them next. In our conversations with God we're in constant danger of doing the same.

We come to worship with our own wants, our own agenda, and our own preconceived notions about what God will be saying to us. That often makes us screen out what God really does have to say. And we cannot heed God's Word if we have not come first of all to listen attentively before we speak.

Therefore Qoheleth instructs: "Let your words be few" (5:2). Jesus gives similar advice when he instructs his disciples, "Do not keep on babbling like pagans, for they think they will be heard because of their many words" (Matt. 6:7). Prayer and praise marathons add little to our worship of God. Jesus reassures us that "Your Father knows what you need before you ask him" (Matt. 6:8).

The Dutch preacher and theologian H. Veltkamp observes in *Zondagskinderen,* his commentary on the Heidelberg Catechism, that more swearing takes place in church than in the bar. The times we take God's name in vain by thoughtlessly and mechanically praying or singing far outnumber the curses echoing through the beer hall. It is that meaningless chatter in our comfortable pew that Qoheleth calls "the sacrifice of fools." It is made up of the offensive offerings of worshipers who so blithely cruise on autopilot that they do not even realize that they do wrong (v. 1) as they roundly insult the living God to his face.

To lend traditional support to this second admonition to "let your words be few" (5:2) before God, Qoheleth attaches a short proverb (5:3) that compares the speech of such a wordy fool to the silly dreams people have when they find themselves under intense stress. Neither makes a lick of sense.

When the tots see Grandpa beckon them to the window, they can be so filled with stories of their own exploits that it does not even register that he's called them in for supper. Then they wonder why Grandpa doesn't feed them. . . .

Mind Your Tongue! (5:4-7)

His third and fourth admonitions (5:4 and 5:6, respectively) provide a concrete example of how our foolish chatter before God can bring us real grief. Unless we guard our tongues, we may foolishly find ourselves making promises to God that we cannot, or will not, keep. Overcome by enthusiasm on the spur of the moment we might forget who we are: limited, finite, weak human beings, who often end up breaking our well-meant promises. That's bad enough when we disappoint each other. But when we spout

off before the Almighty, the stakes increase drastically: "Why should God be angry at what you say and destroy the work of your hands?" (5:6). "It is better not to vow than to make a vow and not fulfil it" (5:5).

Qoheleth's warning (5:6) literally reads, "Do not permit your mouth to bring guilt upon your flesh." The old children's rhyme "Sticks and stones may break my bones but words will never hurt me" is a patent lie. Insults hurt deeply. So do broken commitments. Our words can cause real physical grief, to others and to ourselves as well.

The New Testament writer James minces no words:

The tongue also is a fire, a world of evil among the parts of the body. It corrupts the whole person, sets the whole course of his life on fire, and is itself set on fire by hell.

—*James 3:6*

A wagging tongue can inflict serious injury in church too. The tragedy of Ananias and Sapphira (Acts 5) should caution us that the wider and more informal settings of worship in the New Testament in no way limit the holiness or importance of our meeting with God. Where two or more are gathered in Jesus' name, there he is among them. The indwelling of God's Spirit means that we as living temples come face to face with our Creator wherever we go. When we make our promises to him, he takes us as seriously as he did any pilgrim who actually entered Jerusalem's gate and climbed Mt. Zion to solemnly declare his pledge at the altar in the Holy Place.

We'd better be very careful about the vows we make to God when we make public profession of faith. We'd better tread carefully when we make promises to God at the baptismal font or when we speak the words at our wedding or ordination. God hears our pledges, and he will hold us accountable for each one of them.

We should also tread lightly when we sing in church. Because we so often fail to concentrate on the words we sing, we may easily make promises to God that we will live to regret. Do we really dare to sing a hymn like Thomas O. Chisolm's hymn of dedication, "Living for Jesus"?

Living for Jesus a life that is true, striving to please him in all that I do, yielding allegiance gladhearted and free—this is the pathway of blessing for me. O Jesus, Lord and Savior, I give myself to you, for you in your atonement did give yourself for me. I own no other master—my heart shall be your throne: my life I give, henceforth to live, O Christ, for you alone.

A Christian boys' organization currently adopts this hymn as its theme song. Is that wise? Can we encourage boys ages 9 to 14 to sing this without worrying even a little bit that we may be goading them into hypocrisy, into telling God an enormous fib?

Qoheleth would deem it wiser to sing about what God promises and what God does than to croon about our own good intentions. The road to hell is paved with them. God is in heaven. We are on earth. He always comes through. We don't. Our hymnody should respect that. Qoheleth warns us, "Much dreaming and many words are meaningless. Instead, fear God" (5:7—author's translation).

Derek Kidner, in his commentary on Ecclesiastes, explains this conclusion appropriately and succinctly: ". . . the

dreams appear to be daydreams reducing worship to verbal doodling" (*The Message of Ecclesiastes*, p. 53).

Worship leaders who insist on making us sing the same repetitive choruses over and over again to "really get us to worship God" should check if they are keeping us from doing precisely that. So easily we allow worship to degrade into a form of entertainment by which we try to offer a smorgasbord of goods to please every palate. We let it become "consumer driven" instead of Holy Spirit driven. In his excellent survey of organized religion in Canada, Reginald Bibby warns against worship that offers no more than a constant diet of our own novel ideas:

Religion is more than beliefs, practices, experience, and knowledge. Historically, it has also been a resource. It has had a supernatural component, God. It has also had a social component in the form of a community of believers. The result is that the committed have claimed spiritual and social support as they live out their lives.

When religion is reduced to consumption fragments, it is unlikely to be able to function as such a resource. The supernatural component is fragmented: a relationship with the Divine is reduced to an occasional prayer; the social component is fragmented: participation in a community is replaced by attendance at an occasional service.
—Fragmented Gods, *p. 173*

Qoheleth prescribes the only antidote to worship made meaningless by chasing our own whims and dreams: a healthy dose of godly fear that makes us "all ears" for "what (God) the Spirit says to the churches" (Rev. 2:7, 11, 17, 29; 3:6, 13, 22).

Injustice and Meaningless Wealth Revisited (5:8-20)

After pointing beyond the meaninglessness of our own pious words and noble intentions to a more God-centered form of worship, Qoheleth retraces some of his steps.

He takes up again the theme of oppression and injustice. He has already agonized with us over why God allows it (3:16), shown us that as humans we cannot get much of a handle on it (3:17-21) and that we had best leave the matter in the hands of One who is older and wiser (3:22) than we are. He has wondered out loud if those who were victims of oppression would not be better off dead (4:2-3). He has also identified its root cause: our meaningless envy of our neighbor (4:4).

In today's passage, Qoheleth follows a similar route. His reflection on why there is so much injustice (5:8-9) again leads him back to the cause for it: greed. He expands on this by offering five reasons why such striving for riches is meaningless (5:10-17)—why it's not worth the misery and pain it inflicts on the oppressed. He then reaches the conclusion that by now has become his well-known refrain (5:18-20).

The High and the Mighty (5:8-9)

God instituted the state to maintain justice and freedom. But a quick scan of governments ancient and modern confronts us with the sad fact that the authorities themselves are often the greatest contributors to oppression and inequity. Nebuchadnezzar, the Ptolemies, Caligula, Napoleon, Stalin, Hitler, Hussein—the rogues' parade marches its dreary way on

through history with blood-stained boots stomping out the freedom, rights, and the happiness of "friends" and foes alike.

Don't be surprised, Qoheleth tells us,

for one official is eyed by a higher one,
and over them both are others higher
still. The increase of the land is taken by
all; the king himself profits from the
fields.

(5:8-9)

After the fall, the order in this sinful world has not reflected its created purpose. More often than not we sinful humans twist and distort the legitimate powers and authorities God has delegated to us. That is true in our marriages and families. It's just as true in government.

Why is the state corrupt? Not first of all because the social order is too messed up or because we have not yet found the magic formula for good government. It's bad, Qoheleth states, because the same rat race that takes place in our own lives takes place in the civil service as well.

For our word "official" Qoheleth simply uses three times a Hebrew word that means "high one"—perhaps best translated into current English as "big shot." Verse 8 would then read: ". . . for one big shot is eyed by another big shot, and there are other big shots over them" (5:8).

Qoheleth points out that the system allows so much oppression and injustice because those within it care primarily for themselves. They eye their subordinates, and take their share of the wealth in taxes from the people they are supposed to serve and protect. However, within this sinful world their real concern, quite naturally, is their own gain, not the welfare of the taxpayer. Despite our "advancement" of more than two thousand years of civilization we can still readily identify with this complaint, especially at tax time.

Don't be surprised, Qoheleth tells us, that a good system of government does not turn greedy sinners into altruistic saints. The sinner always perverts the system instead. Regardless of how good the system is, it will never change anything for the better until the heart of every individual is thoroughly cleansed of sin and purged of selfishness and greed. Only God's kingdom offers that possibility. Down here, Winston Churchill's keen observation continues to apply: "Democracy is the worst form of government . . . except for any other form."

Verse 9 somehow continues the picture of governmental self-interest, extending it even to the king. The Hebrew is very obscure, creating insurmountable difficulties for translators and commentators. They understand this verse in a wide variety of ways. If we follow the New International Version, Qoheleth argues that even the king participates in the trickle-up process by which every big shot grabs what he or she can from those beneath him or her from the farmer's hard work (compare 1 Sam. 8:10-18). The engine that keeps the whole government pyramid, from top to bottom, churning on the sweaty backs of the hard-working taxpayer is exactly the same one that makes taxpayers walk all over each other: greed. So once again Qoheleth needs to address the unholy motive that resides in civil servants just as much as in the rest of us (5:10-17).

Five Reasons Not to Be Greedy (5:10-17)

In rapid-fire succession, Qoheleth rattles off five reasons why greed makes our existence so senseless.

1. (5:10) People who love money or profit will never have enough. They will always pine for more.

2. (5:11) The more money people make, the more they have to pay out: employees, overhead, taxes. Why should we work so hard to let others make a living leeching off our successes? Besides, our stomachs will only hold so much. When we have more than we need, all we can do with the rest of it is watch it grow and eventually see it vaporize into thin air.

3. (5:12) The more wealth one has, the bigger and more numerous the headaches it precipitates. After a hard day's work in the field the laborer sleeps soundly. But tension-filled pencil pushing and high-pressure decision-making keep the rich slaving into the wee hours. Even then sleep won't come easily to an overstressed mind. Tired muscles grant the worker an enjoyable snooze, but an exhausted mind denies the rich even that happiness, keeping them at their toil even in their dreams.

4. (5:13-14) Riches do not guarantee greater happiness, nor do they insulate their owner from suffering. Qoheleth observes:

I have seen a grievous evil under sun: wealth hoarded to the harm of its owner or wealth lost through some misfortune, so that when he has a son there is nothing left for him.
                                   (5:13-14)

Wealth can cause injury in many ways. It can isolate us from others, destroy relationships, cause us mental and emotional anguish (5:12), and subject us to robbery, extortion, and any number of other life-shattering experiences.

And because it's here today, gone tomorrow, its loss can cause incredible pain. Better to be poor all one's life than to taste the good life and suddenly have to give it up. Even the small, fleeting joy of leaving something to the kids (2:21) will be rudely torn away, leaving nothing but an aching void.

5. (5:15-17) The baby-boomers are heading into their forties. The generation that imagined itself unstoppable and invincible now shudders at the fearful realization of its own mortality. The gray hairs and "spare tire" testify to the falsehood of the "forever young" songs on which they grew up. Qoheleth again reminds us that even if we manage to hang on to our wealth through thick and thin, death will strip away every last dime for which we have struggled and sacrificed so much. How senselessly we suffer and cause suffering for what just evaporates into thin air!

Enjoy Your Wealth (5:18-20)

Having shown how meaningless the love of wealth and the struggle to achieve and hoard it are, Qoheleth reminds us that wealth in and of itself is not bad. Whatever we possess, much or little, it is a gift from God's hand. We need only to recognize our limits. We need to enjoy what our Provider gives and not sacrifice our happiness by struggling to seize or latch on to what he has decided to give us only in his own good time, for as short or as long as he considers appropriate.

Jesus teaches us to pray, "Give us *today* our daily bread" (Matt. 6:11). And that's enough. The same heavenly Father who looks after our needs today will be there for us tomorrow. Trust in him makes us as free as the birds to live from one day to the next seeking "first his kingdom and his righteousness." We're sure that "all these things will be given to [us] as well," since our "heavenly Father knows that we need them" (Matt. 6:32-33). Jesus confirms the Teacher's wisdom:

Therefore, do not worry about tomorrow, for tomorrow will worry about itself. Each day has enough trouble of its own.
—Matthew 6:34

God-Ordered Frustration (6:1-12)

"God wants you to be successful," the televangelists scream at us. "Dare to make God your business partner and you'll be rolling in dough."

Great! Thanks for the boost. It's not bad enough that I've got the creditors after my hide; now I'm told that I'm at fault for my own financial collapse: I don't have enough faith. Just what I need to hear. Now I'm not only cash poor, but I'm made to believe that my faith life isn't worth a plugged nickel either!

Qoheleth emphatically dismisses this simplistic theology of success. He's much too keen an observer to be led by the nose:

God gives a man wealth, possessions, and honor, so that he lacks nothing his heart desires, but God does not enable him to enjoy them, and a stranger enjoys them instead.
(6:2)

Notice it is God himself who ordains this meaningless, grievous evil. He may well dangle success in front of us with the one hand and immediately rob us of any joy it might bring with the other. Why? Qoheleth cannot say. Like Job, he does not receive any soul-satisfying answers, but he refuses to toe the line of traditional wisdom that maintained that

God only does these things to punish people who have crossed him. Qoheleth can only observe that these things are so and agonize over their apparent absurdity. All he can offer is the conclusion that a stillborn child would be better off than we are. At least such a child never experienced the frustration of having nothing while having it all. Even Qoheleth's own refrain, advising us that we should enjoy what God gives us (5:18-20), has its God-ordained limits.

Nothing we do can change the lot in life that God apportions to us: not gorging ourselves (6:7), earning a sheepskin (6:8), or even playing our cards right (6:8). The best we can do is to content ourselves with whatever happiness God does throw our way (6:9) and keep our roving appetites for more in check.

The Greek philosopher Epicurus strongly echoed this advice. He taught that we should not cultivate our tastes but rest content with a simple loaf of bread and a chunk of cheese. These things we can probably afford throughout our lives. The problem with acquiring richer tastes lies in the fact that our chances of continually filling them drastically decrease. And if we become accustomed to steak and lobster, bread and cheese will no longer do, even though that is all we can afford. Unfortunately for the memory of Epicurus, his name has become firmly associated with the very thing he taught against: unbridled gluttony and sensuousness. Wise Epicurus would roll over in his grave if he knew!

Qoheleth ends his reflection on God's apportioning of wealth and poverty, enjoyment and frustration, by advising us not to beat our heads against the wall by rebelling against our Maker:

Whatever exists has already been named, and what man is has been known; no man can contend with One who is stronger than he.

(6:10)

And the more we bellyache, the less sensibly we speak: "The more the words, the less the meaning, and how does that profit anyone?" (6:11).

No, Qoheleth reminds us, we do not know what is good for us in our fleeting lives down here. Nor do we know what it will mean after we're gone (6:12). But if we really trust God, we won't need to know. We'll accept the fact that he has his (good) reasons. And that's enough.

The tots think it's pretty mean of Grandpa to call them in from the yard when they are just having so much fun. And then he sticks them in the bathtub to boot! But Grandpa knows best. Despite their hollering and complaining, deep down they know that.

CHAPTER SEVEN

Live Within the Limits

A good name is better than fine
  perfume,
and the day of death better
  than the day of birth.
It is better to go to a house of mourning
  than to go to a house of feasting,
for death is the destiny of every man;
  the living should take this to heart.
Sorrow is better than laughter,
  because a sad face is good for the
  heart.
The heart of the wise is in the house of
  mourning,
  but the heart of fools is in the house of
  pleasure.
It is better to heed a wise man's rebuke
  than to listen to the song of fools.
Like the crackling of thorns under the
  pot,
  so is the laughter of fools.
This too is meaningless.

Extortion turns a wise man into a fool,
  and a bribe corrupts the heart.

The end of a matter is better than its
  beginning,
and patience is better than pride.
Do not be quickly provoked in your spirit,
  for anger resides in the lap of fools.

Do not say, "Why were the old
  days better than these?"
  For it is not wise to ask such
questions.

Wisdom, like an inheritance, is a good
  thing
  and benefits those who see the sun.
Wisdom is a shelter
  as money is a shelter,
but the advantage of knowledge is this:
  that wisdom preserves the life of its
  possessor.

Consider what God has done:

Who can straighten
  what he has made crooked?
When times are good, be happy;
  but when times are bad, consider:
God has made the one
  as well as the other.
Therefore, a man cannot discover
  anything about his future.

In this meaningless life of mine I have
seen both of these:

a righteous man perishing in his righteousness,

and a wicked man living long in his
      wickedness.
Do not be overrighteous,
      neither be overwise—
      why destroy yourself?
Do not be overwicked,
      and do not be a fool—
      why die before your time?
It is good to grasp the one
      and not let go of the other.
The man who fears God will avoid all
      extremes.

Wisdom makes one wise man more pow-
      erful
      than ten rulers in a city.

There is not a righteous man on earth
      who does what is right and never sins.

Do not pay attention to every word peo-
      ple say,
      or you may hear your servant cursing
      you—
for you know in your heart
      that many times you yourself have
      cursed others.

All this I tested by wisdom and I said,

"I am determined to be wise"—
      but this was beyond me.
Whatever wisdom may be,
      it is far off and most profound—
      who can discover it?
So I turned my mind to understand,
      to investigate and to search out wis-
      dom and the scheme of things
and to understand the stupidity of
      wickedness
      and the madness of folly.

I find more bitter than death
      the woman who is a snare,
whose heart is a trap

and whose hands are chains.
The man who pleases God will escape
      her,
      but the sinner she will ensnare.

"Look," says the Teacher, "this is what I
have discovered:

"Adding one thing to another to discover
      the scheme of things—
      while I was still searching
      but not finding—
I found one upright man among a thou-
      sand,
      but not one upright woman among
      them all.
This only have I found:
      God made mankind upright,
      but men have gone in search of many
      schemes."

Who is like the wise man?
Who knows the explanation of things?
Wisdom brightens a man's face
      and changes its hard appearance.
      —Ecclesiastes 7:1-8:1

After retracing his steps down the path of riches and wealth, Qoheleth once again strikes out on the path of wisdom. He has already concluded that the pursuit of wisdom brings sorrow (1:18) and no lasting meaning (2:15). Yet he has found this pursuit to have real—although limited—value for the time that we are alive (2:13-14) because it helps us to make the most of the times and seasons God gives us (3:11-14).

Qoheleth now wanders again down wisdom's way, probing once more its strengths and weaknesses, intrigued by the value-within-limits that wisdom displays. Basically it seems to be on the right track (7:11) and yet somehow it is fundamentally and unavoidably incomplete (7:13-14, 24). He finds wisdom's pleasant trail once again breaking off abruptly at the fence, beyond which even his own teachers cannot take him.

As Far as It Goes

In 7:1-6 Qoheleth quotes with approval a number of traditional wisdom sayings, then points out their limitations in 7:7. He repeats the process in 7:8-10, which leads him to observe in 7:11-12 that wisdom indeed gives us some relative advantage. He then immediately reminds us of our ever-present limits (7:13-14) before showing us that what goes for wisdom also holds for righteous living and maintaining a good reputation (7:1, 15-22): they're worthwhile, but only relatively so. He then recounts how his quest for wisdom and righteousness ended ultimately in failure (7:23-28), leading him no further than the painful, ugly riddle of humanity's self-chosen, fallen state. And yet, even that discovery won't let him give up on wisdom altogether: at least "Wisdom brightens a man's face and changes its hard appearance" (8:1). That's at least worth *something. . . .*

To Counter the Crackling of Thorns (7:1-6)

Sometimes we see things better from a distance than close up. Astronauts circling our planet at a distance of a 120 miles readily perceive what we cannot see down here: how completely insignificant our accomplishments as human beings really are. Except for some stretches of the Great Wall of China and the twinkle of city lights at night, they cannot even see with the naked eye that intelligent life exists on our planet.

Imagine that: thousands of years of sweat and toil, billions of us at it every day and long into the night, with nothing to show for it beyond the confines of Spaceship Earth but some stray radio transmissions advertising underarm deodorant or nasal spray. If extraterrestrial, intelligent life exists, no wonder they leave us alone.

From an astronaut's perspective, we see how incredibly small we are. Not even the sum total of all the output of hundreds, maybe thousands, of generations of human workers has left any significant, visible sign of our presence. Each one of us makes up only one-five-billionth of the present population, and, like the billions who came before us, we disappear again within a cosmic split second. From that orbital perspective, a mere 1/2000th of a light-second away, we realize how incredibly picayune our lives and our personal accomplishments really are.

It is precisely this realization of our own finitude that Qoheleth commends when he quotes the startling and sobering fact that "the day of death is better than the day of birth" (7:1), and that it is better to go to a funeral than a wedding (7:2). He does not need a space-shuttle ride to glimpse this wider perspective. The nearest funeral parlor provides just as good a window.

When we bounce a brand-new baby in our arms or whoop it up at a wedding reception, we may be forgiven for feeling immortal and on top of the world. But in our saner moments we should drop the grand illusion that happy endings go on forever and that tomorrow will always come. A funeral helps us regain a more realistic perspective.

A chastened outlook (7:5) will help us discard the cheap, shallow, party-animal revelry that Qoheleth calls "the crackling of thorns under the pot" (7:6). Such noisy merriment calls lots of attention to itself, but it provides precious little real warmth. No, says, Qoheleth, better a good name (7:1) and a sober, realistic point of view:

Greater good [is] sorrow than laughter because a sad face [makes for] a good heart.

(7:3—author's translation)

We should not misunderstand. Neither Qoheleth nor the traditional wisdom he cites mean to rain on our parade. Both voices merely warn us away from senselessly squandering the precious time we have in this transitory life of ours. Far from being spoilsports, they show us the path to real, genuine joy that comes not from downing another six-pack, but from celebrating the happiness only God can put deep down in our hearts (2:24-26; 7:13-14). With Psalm 90, Qoheleth encourages us to pray: "Teach us to number our days aright, so that we may gain a heart of wisdom" (Ps. 90:12).

So far so good. Qoheleth agrees with the wisdom of the (s)ages. But, as he demonstrated before, their wisdom has its limits, and here he names just two:

Extortion turns a wise man into a fool, and a bribe corrupts the heart.

(7:7)

In any normal situation, properly cultivated wisdom works well enough. But when pushed to extremes, it rapidly breaks down. When pinned to the ropes by violent force, wise people act just like fools do. We can rationally agree in our cozy Sunday evening discussion groups that we should never give in to the demands of kidnappers—prudent conclusion, no doubt! But when the clipped

voice on the other side of the horn threatens to snuff out the life of our baby, such wise generalizations lose all meaning. We've just been reduced to thinking with our guts—like any fool.

The opposite extreme leads to a similar breakdown of wisdom. We all know it's sheer lunacy for people to accept bribes. But with that crisp one-hundred-dollar bill burning in our hand, wisdom quickly yields to rationalization: "What could it hurt . . . just this once?" No, Qoheleth offers, wisdom works well enough, but only within those God-imposed limits of the normal, the average, and the mundane.

Forget the Good Old Days (7:8-10)

Again Qoheleth approvingly quotes some wise words: "The end of a matter is better than its beginning" (7:8). Makes sense. We'd much rather have our business safely completed and taken care of than to start out not knowing how, or even if, we'll *ever* get it done. At the end of the trail we may have to lick some wounds, but satisfaction only comes with a job well done. All's well that ends well.

Traditional wisdom is on a roll now, so Qoheleth rattles off one proverb after another in typical schoolboy fashion: "Patience is better than pride" (8:8); keep your cool because "anger resides in the lap of fools" (8:9); "Do not say, 'Why were the old days better than these?' For it is not wise to ask such questions" (8:10).

WHOA! Where did that last one come from? Certainly not from traditional wisdom—even though Qoheleth gives that impression. He uses the same tone, the same form, and probably, if we could see him, has the same pious, sanctimonious look on his mug.

Qoheleth snuck that one right in there. It almost got past us. He warns us to be careful because traditional wisdom, for all its value, can put us badly out of touch with the present. It may all too easily make us wallow in useless nostalgia for the good old days, when the wise guys always took the medals. But that kind of thinking just tempts us to try to wind back God's clock again, luring us once more into the foolishness he's warned us about in Chapter 3:1-15.

Back to the Fence (7:11-14)

So, even though on the surface Qoheleth seems merely to echo his teachers, he subtly hauls the fence into his conclusion:

Wisdom, like an inheritance, is a good thing and benefits those who see the sun. Wisdom is a shelter as money is a shelter, but the advantage of knowledge is this: that wisdom preserves the life of its possessor.

(7:11-12)

Note well the *limited* value of wisdom: like an inheritance it *won't* last forever, and it's good *only* for the time we continue to see the sun. Like money, we *cannot* take it with us. And though "wisdom makes one wise man more powerful than ten rulers in a city" (7:19), it can only stave off death for so long and can tell us nothing about what will happen next.

Consider what God has done: Who can straighten what he has made crooked? When times are good, be happy; but when times are bad, consider: God has made the one as well as the other.

Therefore, a man cannot discover anything about his future.

(7:13-14)

Avoiding Extremes (7:15-22)

As he continues to examine the value of pursuing wisdom, Qoheleth injects two other concerns into his discussion: the pursuit of righteousness and the pursuit of a good reputation. It's as if he's hopping between three paths at once. He can do so because they all run parallel. What applies to wisdom applies equally to virtue and to achieving a good name: they all have value, but only within their God-ordained limits. Therefore, we should not put all our eggs in any one of these baskets either. Obsessively chasing one of them will only add to our list of previous failures to gain anything lasting and important from our efforts (1:13; 2:1; 2:8; 3:17-18; 4:16; 5:1).

Neither Overrighteous nor Overwise (7:15-18)

Qoheleth begins with an observation:

In this meaningless life of mine I have seen both of these: A righteous man perishing in his righteousness, and a wicked man living long in his wickedness.

(7:15)

He immediately attaches the conclusion he draws from this:

Do not be overrighteous, neither be overwise—why destroy yourself? Do not be overwicked, and do not be a fool—why die before your time?

(7:16-17)

In a world more perfect than ours, good would always be rewarded and evil would always be punished. Unfortunately, Qoheleth observes, life is not like that. On this sinful, fallen planet, moral purity and uprightness will not guarantee success. If we're naive enough to make that assumption, we could be making a fatal mistake. We'd better recognize the sad fact that sometimes "good" boys and girls are murdered in concentration camps while their executioners party into their nineties.

Psychologists have shown a startling picture in miniature of lethal "overrighteousness." They isolated baby rats and raised them on a strict stimulus-response regimen. Every time the rats did the right thing, they received a food pellet. Every time they did the wrong thing, they received a painful jolt from an electrode. Through this orderly system of rewards and punishments the rats soon learned to behave "perfectly."

Unfortunately for the rats, scientists are not paid just to attend to the comforts of rodents. So one day the rats found themselves dumped unceremoniously in an untrained colony of their peers and left to fend for themselves. In this "real world" environment they did not always receive the expected reward for good behavior. In fact, most of the time, the bad behavior exhibited by other rats stole from them the rewards they thought they deserved. The trained rats could not cope with this amoral life. Out of sheer frustration they simply dropped dead.

Qoheleth warns us that the same may happen to us if we place our faith in our own virtue. Life will not reward us for seeking our salvation in our own moral purity and devotion to duty.

Nor will God! God does not offer grace to the self-righteous who waste their precious time putting themselves through the spiritual laundry. Grace is given only to self-acknowledged, dirty sinners who repentantly confess their own crying need and seek the cleansing only the Lamb of God can provide.

Those who think their own righteousness will save them already fail before they start, Qoheleth points out, because "There is not a righteous man on earth who does what is right and never sins" (7:20). To prove it, he records the highly disappointing results of his careful investigation:

I found one upright man among a thousand, but not one upright woman among them all. This only have I found: God made mankind upright, but men have gone in search of many schemes.

(7:28-29)

Qoheleth's point is *not* some male chauvinist notion that men may be bad but women are worse. The structure of the Hebrew lines indicates his real intent: to drop from one to zero, from the smallest possible amount to none, from really bad to worse. This simply emphasizes the fact that whatever our gender, we're all in the same boat: we all lack the righteousness we need to succeed before God. And it's not God's fault. Our Creator made us good. We've brought this brokenness upon ourselves (7:29).

It's not God's fault that those who fight dirty gain a real advantage over those who won't. It's not God's fault that the moral structure in this world has been shattered (for now). So we'd better face up to the reality of evil and deal with it. Rather than looking to our own righteousness to save us, we'd better look elsewhere . . . to the fear (humble, respectful obedience) of One who comes to us from beyond the sun (7:18b).

To clear up the mistaken notion that we should ditch righteous living altogether, Qoheleth reminds us that wickedness and foolishness will put us into the same coffin as trying too hard to be (self) righteous. In this life, righteousness, like wisdom, offers us real, but limited value. Qoheleth's observation that sometimes good gets rewarded with evil and evil with good remains the exception, not the rule. Although idealistic, picky, overly demanding phariseeism presents one lethal extreme, crawling back into the manure pit of our own stupid wickedness presents the other. Like oars in a rowboat, to get anywhere in life

It is good to grasp the one and not let go of the other. The man who fears God will avoid all extremes.

(7:18)

What's in a Good Name? (7:1, 20-22)

If we can find only limited value in wisdom and in virtue, how about in maintaining a sterling reputation? Granted, "there is not a righteous man on earth who does what is right and never sins," (7:20), and we know only too well our own faults and failures. But how about keeping up appearances? Any great advantage in polishing up our image? If we cannot airbrush out the stains on our souls, can't we at least hide them to fool others into *believing* we're picture perfect?

Traditional wisdom certainly saw some real value in that. Qoheleth even agrees: "A good name is better than fine perfume . . ." (7:1). The Hebrew allows for playful simplicity, since the word for "name" looks almost the same as the word for "perfume." Transliterated it

reads: "*tov sem missemen tov*" —"good name [rather] than perfume good."

From the time we are knee-high to grasshoppers our parents pump it into us: keep up appearances. "What will the neighbors think when you squabble like that?" "Sit still and stop squirming in the pew or people will notice!" "What will the teacher think if you go to school in that outfit?"

We worry constantly about what others think. We carefully monitor our every word and action. We torture ourselves for hours in front of the mirror. We spend a big chunk of our paycheck on new outfits to hide the cellulite and on cosmetics to camouflage the bags under our eyes. We'll deny our own pain, we'll hurt our own conscience, we'll sacrifice our own deepest wishes—all because of what others might think. Is it worth it?

Come on, Qoheleth gently chides, don't get so carried away. A good name is better than smelling good. But it's not the be-all and end-all:

Do not pay attention to every word people say, or you may hear your servant cursing you—for you know in your heart that many times you yourself have cursed others.

(7:21-22)

If it really matters so much what others think of you, then you're doomed before you start. No matter how sanitized your reputation and how perfect your image, people will always talk behind your back. The better you look, the more they'll criticize. Do you deny it? Be honest and admit how many times you have done the same thing to that classmate who looks like a million bucks or the competitor who actually cleared that much in a single year.

Let them talk. What others think isn't nearly as important as what God thinks. The apostle Paul writes:

I want men everywhere to lift up holy hands in prayer, without anger or disputing. I also want women to dress modestly, with decency and propriety, not with braided hair or gold or pearls or expensive clothes, but with good deeds, appropriate for women who profess to worship God.

—1 Timothy 2:9-10

Let's drop the pretence and the anxiety about what others think. Keeping a good reputation has some value; it's better than needlessly feeding the gossip mill. But reputation is not what life is all about. The idol "Image" demands too great a sacrifice: our integrity and our God-given peace of mind. Does it matter if our looks, actions, or words set some tongues wagging? In Christ we're God's children, and he thinks the world of us (Matt. 18:10). That's what really counts!

Snares and Chains (7:23-8:1)

So what has Qoheleth learned from all this path-hopping in wisdom's ways? Not a lot. When he adds it all up (7:27), what he has found out easily fits inside a shopping bag:

All this I have tested by wisdom; I said, "I will be wise"; but it was far from me. That which is, is far off, and deep, very deep; who can find it out?

(7:23-24 RSV)

About the grand mysteries of the universe, of why we are here and where we are headed and what will be after us, wisdom remains silent. Although knowledge in our day and age doubles every few years, not all the nuclear accelerators and electron microscopes in the world can tell us why we are here or where we are going after we die. Although most cosmologists still cling tentatively to some kind of "Big Bang" theory of the universe's beginning, they readily admit that we can never answer the question: What was there *before* the Big Bang? The laws of physics, which we rely on to hazard such guesses, simply break down under those primeval conditions. Scientists, like the rest of us, can only shrug their shoulders when facing such ultimate questions.

These are disappointing results, Qoheleth admits. But he's learned something at least, however insignificant:

I find more bitter than death the woman who is a snare, whose heart is a trap and whose hands are chains. The man who pleases God will escape her.

(7:26)

Pity the poor guy who falls for a girl who runs his life as soon as she lands him. A henpecked husband locked into that kind of slavery is better off dead. A ball and chain was certainly not in God's plan for marriage.

But let's also admit that God is equally displeased with a situation where women are so dispossessed of any real say that their only recourse is to manipulate men. Such women can only get cooperation from their partners when they lure them into such a trap. It's no picnic to be reduced to wheedling, whining, plodding, conniving to get somewhere.

God created women and men to live in harmony—in full, equal partnership. God gave Adam "a suitable helper" (Gen. 2:20). The word "helper" has often been interpreted to imply subordination. However, precisely the same word is used of God, who is the helper of Israel. Actually, "suitable helper" is best translated as "colleague" or "partner." In order to restore God's purpose for the sexes to the genuine renewal that Christ bought with his blood, Paul teaches us:

Submit to one another out of reverence for Christ, wives to your husbands as to the Lord . . . and husbands, love your wives, just as Christ loved the church and gave himself up for her. . . .
—*Ephesians 5:21ff*

Qoheleth is saying nothing new when he observes that a relationship can go so badly wrong that one is better off without it. Proverbs tells us that it is "better to live on a corner of the roof than share a house with a quarrelsome wife" (Prov. 21:9). Undoubtedly the same applies to a wife who must put up with a quarrelsome husband.

What is new here is where this observation takes the Teacher. This one example leads him to the assertion that there are precious few upright people in the world (7:28), and that this devastating reality is not God's fault but our own:

This only have I found: God made mankind upright, but men have gone in search of many schemes.

(7:29)

If that is all wisdom teaches him, no wonder it brings Qoheleth nothing but grief (1:18). And yet, painful as it is, that distressing result has incredible value! Knowing our own unrighteousness and guilt, and knowing that our wisdom is so restricted that we cannot resolve these things by ourselves, leads us to look for help elsewhere:

Consider what God has done: Who can straighten what he has made crooked? When times are good, be happy; but when times are bad, consider: God has made the one as well as the other.

(7:13-14)

We will then avoid the extremes that we go to when we attempt to save ourselves. And we will be content simply to fear God—to trust, to heed, to accept God's grace.

Only when the children really see how filthy they got themselves, will they let Grandpa stick them in the tub.

CHAPTER EIGHT

Playing Politics

Obey the king's command, I say, because you took an oath before God. Do not be in a hurry to leave the king's presence. Do not stand up for a bad cause, for he will do whatever he pleases. Since a king's word is supreme, who can say to him, "What are you doing?"

Whoever obeys his command will come to no harm,
    and the wise heart will know the proper time and procedure.
For there is a proper time and procedure for every matter,
    though a man's misery weighs heavily upon him.

Since no man knows the future,
    who can tell him what is to come?
No man has power over the wind to contain it;
    so no one has power over the day of his death.
As no one is discharged in time of war,
    so wickedness will not release those who practice it.

All this I saw, as I applied my mind to everything done under the sun. There is a time when a man lords it over others to his own hurt. Then too, I saw the wicked buried—those who used to come and go from the holy place and receive praise in the city where they did this. This too is meaningless.

When the sentence for a crime is not quickly carried out, the hearts of the people are filled with schemes to do wrong. Although a wicked man commits a hundred crimes and still lives a long time, I know that it will go better with God-fearing men, who are reverent before God. Yet because the wicked do not fear God, it will not go well with them, and their days will not lengthen like a shadow.

There is something else meaningless that occurs on earth: righteous men who get what the wicked deserve, and wicked men who get what the righteous deserve. This too, I say, is meaningless. So I commend the enjoyment of life, because nothing is better for a man under the sun than to eat and drink and be glad. Then joy will accompany him in his work all the days of the life God has given him under the sun.

When I applied my mind to know wisdom and to observe man's labor on earth—his eyes not seeing sleep day or night—then I saw all that God has done. No one can comprehend what goes on

69

under the sun. Despite all his efforts to search it out, man cannot discover its meaning. Even if a wise man claims he knows, he cannot really comprehend it.
—*Ecclesiastes 8:2-17*

Question: What do you call a boatload of politicians and lawyers at the bottom of the ocean?

Current Answer: A good start.

Civil religion has fallen on very hard times. The old faith in political institutions and the rule of law has degenerated into deep skepticism. Bungling and cover-ups at the highest government levels, justice delayed for years in a hopelessly clogged court system, police officers so frustrated they resort to the law of the jungle—these all drain away our confidence that we live in a fundamentally just society.

In Qoheleth's day the situation was no different. Ruled with an iron fist by a foreign dictator, the Israelites had long ago tossed out the grandiose illusion that "the system" was basically sound and worthy and good.

And yet, though it shared this negative view, traditional wisdom had much to say about politics. It did not pretend to suggest that involvement in public service would bring about a new and better world order. But it did suggest that one could play the political game to one's own advantage. That relative good was at least attainable (8:2-5). Keep your nose clean and your head down. Play your cards right, and you'll at least advance yourself, if not the good of the nation.

Qoheleth doubts it. Dashing even this small hope offered by traditional wisdom, he contends that there is no guarantee at all that such wise political maneuvering

will get us even that much. All our hard-won achievements in the public arena just get swept away on someone else's arbitrary whim (8:4, 7). So don't bet the horse ranch on that either.

Qoheleth does not say that all politicians and lawyers are crooked. Far from it. But he does observe that there are bad ones (8:9-11) and that the system does not necessarily turf them out. In fact, the evil ones all too often do well because their ruthlessness and willingness to operate outside of the rules gives them a distinct advantage. Hard work, decency, honesty, and loyalty are no guarantees for political success. That's a bitter pill to swallow, one we keep choking on even today.

Don't bother appealing it to the Highest Court either, he advises. To be sure, God will somehow balance the scales of justice (8:12-13), but in this life we won't necessarily see how (8:14), and the whole business remains well beyond our ability to understand (8:16-17). Best to enjoy life as God gives it rather than gamble away such enjoyment on the thin hope that playing politics will permanently increase our well-being (8:15).

Due Process (8:2-5)

Qoheleth begins by agreeing with traditional wisdom: Obey the king. Do it out of conscience, because you promised God (8:1), and also because, if you don't, the king will squish you like a bug (8:3-4).

In Qoheleth's time, just like today, high-placed civil servants had to take an oath of office. Unlike today, they did not only pledge to do a good job on behalf of the public, they also had to pledge complete and unquestioning obedience to their sovereign. In both instances, these vows were made "so help me God." Although Qoheleth had no love for the dictator ruling his country from across the Nile, he recognized that a vow made directly to God should be kept (5:4). Lying to him would invite certain disaster.

Qoheleth attaches a second reason to obey the king. The Hebrew in verse three is unclear, and different versions translate it in a variety of ways. The NIV's rendering suggests Qoheleth discourages us from joining some kind of "bad cause," perhaps a revolt or plot to overthrow the king. Such attempts usually fail because the king can "do as he pleases"; he has the upper hand.

The RSV translates verse three in such a way that Qoheleth warns us to obey the king with all due haste even if he sends us on an unpleasant mission. Both make good sense, but the Hebrew is just too ambiguous to decide.

However, what is clear is the phrase: "for he [the king] will do whatever he pleases." Whatever it is that one should or should not do when in the king's presence, the fact that he has absolute power means that one should obey first and ask questions later (8:4).

He quotes a proverb to bolster his case:

Whoever obeys (the king's) command will come to no harm, and the wise heart will know the proper time and procedure.

(8:5)

But hold on! Qoheleth says. Doesn't that overstate the case? You have a better chance of keeping your head by obeying rather than rebelling. But can you really be so confident that blind obedience will protect you? Is it really true that you can get your way if you bide your time and patiently follow due process—fill out all the relevant forms in triplicate, pay the

administration fee, and wait your turn in line?

Not on your life! "There is a proper time and procedure for every matter," to be sure. But "a man's misery weighs heavily upon him" (8:6). Why?

Since no man knows the future, who can tell him what is to come? No man has power over the wind to contain it; so no one has power over the day of his death. As no one is discharged in time of war, so wickedness will not release those who practice it.

(8:7-8)

By all means be politically astute, Qoheleth advises. By waiting for the right moment you may just succeed where others fail. By following the right procedure, you may just pull it off. But realize that all your clever scheming and maneuvering will not guarantee your success. In politics, as in all of life, what's here today is gone tomorrow. No one can ensure that today's success will carry over into tomorrow because no one can anticipate accurately what tomorrow will bring (8:7).

Even if you could, you still might not be able to do a thing about it. The winds of public opinion and political alliance blow where they will, and you cannot control them (8:8a). One minute you're sipping champagne in your limo, the next you're drawing unemployment. One minute you manage to curry favor with the king, the next you get him mad and he reduces you to a statistic (8:8b).

And if you rely on dirty tricks to save your scrawny neck, you'll find that such wickedness will just suck you under like a whirlpool until you drown (8:8b).

Ask your commanding officer for an honorable discharge just as the enemy artillery starts coming in (8:8c). Talk about bad timing! All you'll get out of him is a few choice words you can't teach the kids back home. Similarly, Qoheleth argues, don't think you can slink up to the devil, cap in hand, and ask him politely to please let you get back to a nice, pious life now that your little pact with evil has paid off so handsomely. You're in for a very hard time if you turn your back on the partners-in-crime who levered you into power in the first place.

Counterpoints (8:9-11)

If we need proofs for Qoheleth's position that politics provides no hope of lasting success, he's glad to provide them.

First of all, he argues, under the sun we need not wait long to find "a time when a man lords it over others to his own hurt" (8:9). Even gunning for the top job will not do. Should you be "lucky" enough to get it, you may still find that pushing others around hurts you as much as it hurts them. A commentator on American presidential politics observed: "Power corrupts, and absolute power corrupts absolutely."

Qoheleth knew that. How does one gain office without selling one's soul? Besides, the more powerful the politicians, the more powerful the enemies who watch carefully for their chance to move in for the kill. And the bigger the fish, the harder it lands.

A second example of deep trouble on capitol hill: the real stinkers often get the honor—not only in life, but even in death (8:10). So much for integrity in the system: what a meaningless business, Qoheleth complains (8:10b)!

In Qoheleth's day one's fondest dream was of a fancy funeral. The more weeping and wailing of mourners, the better was one's reputation and the more

respected was one's memory. A good name meant a lot (7:1). But history is as fickle as life. All too often it attaches to the memory of renegades the honor that saints deserve while branding genuinely decent people as witless rogues. No percentage in seeking office if your real desire is to achieve a good reputation! Many fine politicians have gone down in history as bunglers while the cutthroats who stabbed them in the back have been hailed forever after as real heroes.

A third example Qoheleth cites to remind us not to expect too much from our toil in the public arena is the problem of delayed justice. Even when rulers do their level best, the system so easily bogs down. Justice gets delayed, and people try to get away with murder. "When the sentence for a crime is not quickly carried out, the hearts of the people are filled with schemes to do wrong" (8:11). The problem of a clogged justice system snowballs. A small let-up in dealing effectively with crime encourages more crime that makes it even harder to cope and encourages even more criminal activity. Even the most rigidly ordered societies display this inherent instability. The sudden breakup of the U.S.S.R., unimaginable a few short years ago, clearly illustrates how any society, even the most tightly controlled, is never more than a few steps away from spiralling into complete chaos and internal collapse.

What good is the rule of law if we cannot enforce it? Bleeding hearts who argue that criminals need treatment, not punishment, are as sadly mistaken as those who naively believe that a "get-tough" response will solve our problems. Qoheleth argues that there really *are* "bad" people, not just maladjusted ones. Not all the treatment in the world can cure them unless the Wounded Healer himself lances their hearts with his razor-sharp Word, drains the filth from within, and cleanses the incision with his own blood. Until that happens, none of our own attempts at correction or prevention will really succeed; neither the kid gloves nor the iron fist will do.

Before the Supreme Court (8:12-13)

Qoheleth's dialogue with his teachers continues. All right, they concede, maybe here on earth acting wisely and prudently within public life does not guarantee any lasting gain. But surely acting rightly and justly will help us in the highest court-room of all: God's! Qoheleth agrees. I know, I know, he stammers. Somehow it must:

Although a wicked man commits a hundred crimes and still lives a long time, I know that it will go better with God-fearing men, who are reverent before God. Yet because the wicked do not fear God, it will not go well with them, and their days will not lengthen like a shadow.
(8:12-13)

Somehow God's justice must and will prevail. Qoheleth's faith remains unwavering. God will surely balance the scales. But how?

Qoheleth just shrugs. His keen eyes show him that there are "righteous men who get what the wicked deserve, and wicked men who get what the righteous deserve" (8:14). All the wisdom under the sun cannot help him understand what God is up to in dealing in this way with us struggling creatures:

When I applied my mind to know wisdom and to observe man's labor on earth—his

eyes not seeing sleep day or night—then I saw all that God has done. No one can comprehend what goes on under the sun. Despite all his efforts to search it out, man cannot discover its meaning. Even if a wise man claims he knows, he cannot really comprehend it.
(8:16-17)

Faith does not always need answers.

When one of the youngsters keeps bullying the other one, the underdog cannot fathom why Grandpa won't judiciously intervene to put matters right. Grandpa has his reasons, but how does he explain them to a preschooler?

Going Steady with Joy (8:15)

Qoheleth makes no attempt to undercut the importance of our working for true justice in society. Nowhere does he tell us to stop working—and working hard—in this world, in every area of life. We are created in God's image to do precisely that.

But we so easily turn even that godly objective of doing justice into an idol. When we place our faith in a just world order here under the sun, then we badly overestimate our own ability. The Bible clearly reveals that we cannot and will not achieve true justice until Jesus Christ returns to fully usher in his glorious and gentle reign. Former US presidential aide Charles Colson has given a lot of careful thought to this limitation. He warns:

Today's misspent enthusiasm for political solutions to the moral problems of our culture arises from a distorted view of both politics and spirituality—too low a view of the power of a sovereign God and too high a view of the ability of man. The idea that human systems, reformed by

Christian influence, pave the road to the Kingdom—or at least, to revival—has the same utopian ring that one finds in Marxist literature.
—*Kingdoms in Conflict, p. 304*

Until Christ returns, the best we can hope for is to catch glimpses of that kingdom as its first dawning rays steal into the present. But until then these lights remain beacons only, awash in a dark ocean of corruption, intolerance, and injustice.

The reason we work for justice, Qoheleth argues, is not because we need to bring in God's Kingdom with our own ingenuity and goodness. That won't work.

It's simply because we *enjoy* living that way. Transformed by God's power, we choose justice, mercy, and forgiveness over self-advancement. We trust in him to put it all right, even though we have no idea how he will do that. We can forgive and forget and lose 'em *all* because God will surely vindicate us (Matt. 25:31-46). In the meantime we may continue to act justly and work hard politically in God's name because we enjoy it. We love to share with others a taste of the good life that God so freely gives to us:

So I commend the enjoyment of life, because nothing is better for a man under the sun than to eat and drink and be glad. Then joy will accompany him in his work all the days of the life God has given him under the sun.

(8:15)

How sad when we sacrifice our enjoyment of life to the idol of "the perfect human-made society." It won't fly, Qoheleth warns us. Idols never deliver;

they just keel over on their ugly faces and self-destruct. Besides, God has already gift-wrapped the just society. It will be his wedding present to us when we marry the Lamb. So enjoy. Take heart. Colson urges:

Stop. Listen. Over the din of the conflict, if you listen carefully, you will hear the chorus echoing in the distance: "The kingdom of this world has become the kingdom of our Lord and of his Christ."

Listen. For in that glorious refrain is man's one hope.
—*Kingdoms in Conflict, p. 371*

That hope permits God's joy to accompany us in our hard work in the courtroom, the senate chamber, the correctional facility, the consistory room, and wherever our King calls us to play politics.

For Its Own Sake

At the end of MGM movies the lion gives its mighty roar like a parting blessing or a final, denture-rattling "Amen." In the surrounding crest we see emblazoned the company motto: "*Ars gratia artis*": "Art for the sake of art."

In a truly free society, nothing should cheapen true art by forcing it to serve interests outside its own. It has its own God-given area of meaning and value. The state should not demean it by making it generate propaganda. Nor should private enterprise turn it into a legal thief, picking our pockets by making products look so irresistible to us that we buy what we do not need. True art should be produced and enjoyed for its own God-given sake. We should produce "art for the sake of art"—unlike MGM, who seems to

crank out movies for only one purpose: to
make money.

The same holds true for our pursuit of
justice. Qoheleth teaches us that we
should not jump into the public arena
with high-blown dreams of hijacking the
rule of law to build some Paradise on
earth. Nor should we throw our hat into
the ring because we want to squeeze private wealth, power, or fame out of public
life. We should enter public service for
its own sake—because God gave us the
exercise of justice as a means of working
fruitfully and covenantally as his repre-
sentatives, his image-bearers (Gen. 1:27).

Although the fall has badly perverted
this area of life, those who are in Christ
may still find enjoyment in giving the
world a preview of what things will one
day be like when Judgment Day ushers in
a whole new society. Like kids, we will
derive real pleasure out of giving our
friends a sneak peek at that Christ-bought
wedding gift. Until we may fully unwrap
it, we let his justice shine wherever we
can in this dark, dirty world—*for its own
sake*—not to our own glory, but to God's
(Matt. 5:14-16).

CHAPTER NINE

A Joy-Filled Sandwich

So I reflected on all this and concluded that the righteous and the wise and what they do are in God's hands, but no man knows whether love or hate awaits him. All share a common destiny—the righteous and the wicked, the good and the bad, the clean and the unclean, those who offer sacrifices and those who do not.

As it is with the good man,
    so with the sinner;
as it is with those who take oaths,
    so with those who are afraid to take
        them.

This is the evil in everything that happens under the sun: The same destiny overtakes all. The hearts of men, moreover, are full of evil and there is madness in their hearts while they live, and afterward they join the dead. Anyone who is among the living has hope—even a live dog is better off than a dead lion!

For the living know that they will die
    but the dead know nothing;
they have no further reward,
    and even the memory of them is forgotten.
Their love, their hate

and their jealousy have long
    since vanished;
    never again will they have a part
in anything that happens under the sun.

Go, eat your food with gladness, and drink your wine with a joyful heart, for it is now that God favors what you do. Always be clothed in white, and always anoint your head with oil. Enjoy life with your wife, whom you love, all the days of this meaningless life that God has given you under the sun—all your meaningless days. For this is your lot in life and in your toilsome labor under the sun. Whatever your hand finds to do, do it with all your might, for in the grave, where you are going, there is neither working nor planning nor knowledge nor wisdom.

I have seen something else under the sun:

The race is not to the swift
    or the battle to the strong
nor does food come to the wise
    or wealth to the brilliant
    or favor to the learned;
but time and chance happen to them all.

Moreover, no man knows when his
hour will come:

As fish are caught in a cruel net,
*   or birds are taken in a snare,*
so men are trapped by evil times
*   that fall unexpectedly upon them.*
                    —Ecclesiastes 9:1-12

Hebrew writers like Qoheleth knew
about sandwiches—not the ones we eat,
but the ones we read. They used them
extensively in their writing.

Perhaps that statement needs some
explaining.

It was not until halfway through the
eighteenth century that the fourth Earl of
Sandwich discovered the staple that still
carries his name. He made the remarkable
discovery that one could actually slap lots
of good stuff on bread and still eat it in a
fairly refined manner as befitting a
courtier of those nobler days. One needed
only to fold the bread over so that one
could squeeze all the good stuff into the
middle.

Lunchtime at school provides the
opportunity to conduct some major market testing of this interesting creation. It
dawns soon enough on most children that
they can pull the layers of bread apart,
nibble off the peanut butter and jelly
within, and discretely sneak the leftover
bread back into their lunch bucket for
subsequent disposal out of the school bus
window. But sooner or later they forget
the sleight-of-hand phase of the procedure, and a startled parent finds the dis-
gusting, uneaten remains. A lengthy lecture naturally follows on the importance
of maintaining a nutritionally balanced
diet. Frustrated mothers and fathers find
themselves promising virtual immortality
in a continuous state of robust vitality if
the experimenters will just return to the

more acceptable practice of eating the
whole thing: stale, chewy outsides as
well as delectable insides!

Because they did not enjoy the benefits of the Earl of Sandwich's great discovery, Hebrew poets and writers had to
make do with loaves of bread that resembled pizza shells. But they knew about
verbal sandwiches. In their writing they
knew how to put the good stuff on the
inside and the important stuff on the outsides. That's the method they used to signal to us what the real heart of their message was, and they framed that central
truth on both sides with important sup-
porting materials that perfectly balances
our reading diet.

Go for It!

Chapter 9:1-12 gives us a good example of such a verbal sandwich. Qoheleth
begins with an introduction (9:1-2) that
sums up what he has concluded from his
discussion in the previous chapter: all we
do is in God's hands (9:1a); we do not
know what's still in store for us (9:1b);
and we all share a common destiny (9:2).

Having introduced these three themes,
he elaborates on them in the next ten
verses. But he also rearranges them, link-
ing them together in sandwich form:

Bad Part: Reason 1 for Command
                              —9:3-6

Good Part: Command: Enjoy!
                              —9:7-10

Bad Part: Reason 2 for Command
                              —9:11-12

By squeezing his command in
between his two reasons for giving it,
Qoheleth signals for us what he considers
the real heart of the matter. But at the

same time he manages to balance our diet by enabling us to swallow the tough parts as well.

In Good Hands (9:1-2)

In the previous chapter Qoheleth examined the relative merits of public service. He found traditional wisdom's view—that a good grasp of proper timing and procedure could bring success— overly hopeful and unrealistic. He saw too many examples to the contrary. Humans simply do not have enough fore-sight and strength to ensure their political fortunes, no matter how righteous or wise they might be. So he concludes from this "that the righteous and the wise and what they do are in God's hands . . ." (9:1).

Right. That would settle the matter for traditional wisdom: since our fate is in God's hands, human beings can control the outcome; God will always reward good behavior and punish bad. These sages had reduced God to nothing more than a rational/moral system that unswervingly behaves in the same bor-ing, mechanical way. They had trans-formed our Creator into a big justice mill in the sky who cannot rescue murderers from crosses.

Not so Qoheleth, whose keen eye observes a God who is much more com-plicated and free than that. Yes, our lives are completely in God's hand. No, that does not mean we can manipulate God to gain our own way: ". . . no man knows whether love or hate awaits him" (9:1). God may treat a good person hatefully and a bad person lovingly. The Teacher has seen examples of both. Therefore our lives, and our relationship to God, turn out to be much more complex than Qoheleth's teachers had thought. We can-not get any handle on what God has in store for us on this planet.

Also, our "common destiny" levels all distinctions—not only between rich and poor, but also between

the righteous and the wicked, the good and the bad, the clean and the unclean, those who offer sacrifices and those who do not.

(9:2)

Just so the traditionalists get the point (and perhaps to rub it in a little), Qoheleth repeats it:

As it is with the good man, so with the sinner; as it is with those who take oaths, so with those who are afraid to take them.

(9:2)

Reason 1: The Great Leveler Calls Again (9:3-6)

One of the great tombstone inscrip-tions of all time, in a twisted sort of way, reads only

I *TOLD* YOU I WAS SICK.

Had the script been Hebrew and had the grave been located in Palestine instead of England, that tombstone could have been Qoheleth's. He never seems to weary of telling us precisely how sick we are in this fallen world. If he drove a car, it might have sported the common bumper sticker complaint

YOU WORK. YOU PAY TAXES. THEN YOU DIE.

In verse 3, Qoheleth agonizes again over the cruel, evil reality that all people who live under the sun meet the same destiny. It seems so terribly unfair that the good and the bad, the rich and the poor, the religious and the irreligious should all end up the same. In a perfect world there would be no wickedness at all. In a partially fallen world at least good would be rewarded and evil punished. But under the sun we seem to live in the worst of all possible worlds: a world devoid of justice, where our common fate levels all differences and makes everything we do in this life seem hopelessly futile and meaningless.

Qoheleth voices his complaint in almost precisely the same way as the bumper sticker: first characterizing the meaninglessness of this life and then abruptly breaking off in midsentence to drive home the awful suddenness by which death steals even that away from us. Unfortunately both NIV and RSV try to smooth over the angry jerkiness of Qoheleth's Hebrew:

The hearts of men, moreover, are full of evil and there is madness in their hearts while they live, and afterwards . . . THEY DIE!

(9:3—author's translation)

However, this bitter pill that Qoheleth has to swallow does not make him suicidal. True, in chapter 4:2 he told us that "the dead, who had already died, are happier than the living, who are still alive." But there he was not making a comment on human life in general. He was agonizing over the evil reality that the oppressed have no one to comfort them. At least dead people do not have to keep getting their nose rubbed in that misery by continuing to witness it! We have to take his complaint in 4:2 seriously, but in the same way as we take seriously the distraught student who moans "I flunked English; I wish I were dead!" Literalism misses the point.

Qoheleth still sees value in our lives "under the sun." No ultimate value, but value nevertheless. Those who live still have hope (9:4). Good things could still come their way. Besides, the living still know *something*, even if it's only the sobering fact that they will die (9:5). And, as he explains later, that knowledge *does* make a difference (9:7-10).

To prove his point that life has at least this relative value, he muses that "even a live dog is better off than a dead lion!" (9:4b). Dogs in his day were what rats or slugs are in ours: the vilest critters one could think of. Back then the only insult more devastating than calling someone a dog was to call that person a dead dog. A live dog is at least better than a dead one. In fact, Qoheleth observes, a live dog is better off than *any* dead creature, including the magnificent beast the Hebrews already had dubbed "the king of beasts."

Living dogs are also better than dead *people*. The latter have no more reward, no more reputation, and no more passions. They are simply written out of the script (9:5-6); exit, downstage . . . and out.

Reason 2: All Must Roll the Dice (9:11-12)

The ancients liked to have the climax to a story in the middle. They expected the narrator to walk them into the story and then to walk them back out of it again—like eating a sandwich layer by layer. Today we prefer to save the good part until close to the end of the tale, without dragging it out much longer after that—like taking the sandwich apart, eating both slices of bread first, and then helping ourselves to the savory filling for dessert. So, because we live now and not in Qoheleth's time, we'll take up Qoheleth's second complaint first (9:11-12) and save the good part of his story (9:7-10) for last.

Having reminded us of death's leveling effect, Qoheleth now hauls out the second bitter pill we must swallow: even while we live, there seems to be no rhyme or reason to who ends up with what; we have no control over our own lot in life. He voices his complaint in a bitter denial of what his instructors taught him. Against traditional wisdom he stubbornly contends that:

The race is not to the swift or the battle to the strong, nor does food come to the wise or wealth to the brilliant or favor to the learned; but time and chance happen to them all.

(9:11)

More often than not it's the swiftest runner who gets tripped, the best soldier who hits the land mine, the smartest investor who gets caught in the stock tumble, and the best scholar who gets brutally misinterpreted and denounced. We can't assume that careful planning, thorough training, and honest hard work will get us anywhere—and that makes life extremely difficult. Our lives seem to be nothing more than one big roll of the dice. Doesn't seem at all fair. . . .

Moreover, no man knows when his hour will come: As fish are caught in a cruel net, or birds are taken in a snare, so men are trapped by evil times that fall unexpectedly upon them.

(9:12)

We can just be humming along through life when BANG, out of the blue,

the trap snaps shut, and in one split second disaster wipes out all our accomplishments, reducing us to a miserable shell of what we used to be.

Examples are so numerous that Qoheleth does not even bother to mention them: the stroke survivor, the rape victim, the parents returning from vacation with the infant seat now grievously empty. No need to haul in examples from elsewhere . . . just look in the mirror. Sooner or later evil times will trap us all. When they fall, they're always unexpected. And they ruin all our ambitions and hopes.

So Live It Up! (9:7-10)

Two bitter pills to swallow, two dry chunks of realism that stick in our throats. Qoheleth, why are you telling us this? We cannot deny that what you're saying is true. But why don't you leave us cowering in our pretty dreams and brave little plans? It's not so scary here under the bed! Why do you roust us out to make us face the fearsome reality of a broken, sinful world that will all too soon make good its threat to do us in? You tell us we can't run. You show us we can't hide. Do you only want to confront us with this reality so we'll share your deep despair and go out and hang ourselves?

On the contrary! Qoheleth urges. You need to know this so that you will make the most of every chance you still have to really live it up!

Go, eat your bread with enjoyment, and drink your wine with a merry heart; for God has already approved what you do.

(9:7 RSV)

A sandwich made up only of two slices of dry bread is pretty dreary. So is knowing that death will rob us of any further experience or meaning in this world.

So is knowing that the bad times can hit us at any moment. If those are our only certainties in life, then life isn't worth spit.

But that's *not* all there is. Qoheleth points us back to God. There is an eternal, all-powerful, almighty God in control. And that God will take care of his own somehow: "The righteous and the wise and their deeds are in God's hands . . ." (9:1). Whether God has decreed good or ill for us in this life, no one can tell. But Qoheleth knows that God makes plans that never fail—plans that include us. Within that plan God has indeed set limits to prevent us from achieving our own salvation. But God has also given us lots of room to enjoy our lives within those limits—to experience some of the goodness of being human beings, who relish a good meal and savor a glass of fine wine (9:7).

For Qoheleth, the limits serve not to demoralize us, but to point us back to God. God will take care of the big picture. God will do what needs doing. Our Creator has given us lots of time to play and play hard in the creation. "He has already approved what we do" (9:7), Qoheleth writes. God wants us to be happy. So do what God wants! Be happy!

There is nothing more heartbreaking than to see children reduced to slaves. Either out of necessity or out of fear they spend their short, precious childhood years working, fretting, fulfilling responsibility after responsibility, as if they are adults. No loving parents would want such a life for their children. They gladly take care of the problems and work hard to create some room for their children to play, have fun, and enjoy their lives. So does God.

Does God need us to keep the sky up? No. Does God need us to keep the world turning? No. Does God need our skill and craftsmanship to fix this busted world? No. Does God need us to build the church? No. Does God need us to bring in the New Jerusalem? No. All these things God can and will do without our help!

Then what does God need us for? God needs us only to experience, celebrate, and share his tender mercies and his gentle, Fatherly love. So, despite the miseries of a fallen world

Let your garments be always white; let not oil be lacking on your head. Enjoy life with the wife whom you love, all the days of your vain life which he has given you under the sun, because that is your portion in life and in your toil at which you toil under the sun.

(9:8-9 RSV)

God has removed from our backs the heavy burden of achieving our own salvation and the salvation of the world. Jesus shouldered that heavy cross himself in order that we might have abundant life. Our job is simply to make every day a celebration of what God is doing for us. Despite the tears and hurts that will inevitably come our way, our fundamental posture in this world can remain one of rejoicing. Even when our dark depression stretches into months and we're drained of all emotion, feeling, or caring, the "white garments" and "oil on our heads" (9:8) may serve to remind those around us, and ourselves as well, that God will swallow this present darkness up in victory.

Qoheleth goes beyond mentioning wine and oil and white robes. He jolly well expects us to exchange our party hats and dancing shoes every now and then for hard hats and work boots. But

even our hard work must and may remain
a source of pleasure, joy, and celebration.

When parents allow their children to
help with the chores, it's for their kids'
benefit, not their own. Those efforts tend
to contribute little to the family fortunes.
When Susie wants to help with the lawn
mowing, she usually just gets in the way.
When Eric wants to help bake the cake,
he inevitably makes it flop. Parents can
do the job faster and better on their own.
But it's good for kids to putter in the
kitchen and the garden.

It's the same, says Qoheleth, with the
work God gives us to do. God doesn't
need our assistance. It doesn't really help
him much. But he wants it: "Whatever
your hand finds to do, do it with all your
might, for in the grave, where you are
going, there is neither working nor planning nor knowledge nor wisdom" (9:10).

Childhood ends. So does our life
under the sun. So while we have it, we
should make the most of it. God redeems
even our meaningless work, and in the
light of eternity, elevates it to faith-filled
play. Although our deeds will accomplish
nothing, and although they will not out-
last us, they do make a lasting impression
in the memory of God (Rev. 14:13) who
in Christ has already approved them
(9:7). And if God sets limits to remind us
that we are his children, not his slaves,
let's do him the favor and the courtesy of
resting content in his will (as Qoheleth
would say, "accepting our lot").

CHAPTER TEN

Wisdom Stew

I also saw under the sun this example of wisdom that greatly impressed me: There was once a small city with only a few people in it. And a powerful king came against it, surrounded it and built huge siegeworks against it. Now there lived in that city a man poor but wise, and he saved the city by his wisdom. But nobody remembered that poor man. So I said, "Wisdom is better than strength." But the poor man's wisdom is despised, and his words are no longer heeded.

The quiet words of the wise are more to
be heeded
than the shouts of a ruler of fools.
Wisdom is better than weapons of war,
but one sinner destroys much good.
As dead flies give perfume a bad smell,
so a little folly outweighs wisdom and
honor.
The heart of the wise inclines to the right,
but the heart of the fool to the left.
Even as he walks along the road,
the fool lacks sense
and shows everyone how stupid he is.
If a ruler's anger rises against you,
do not leave your post;
calmness can lay great errors to rest.

There is an evil I have seen
under the sun,
the sort of error that arises from
a ruler:
Fools are put in many high positions,
while the rich occupy the low ones.
I have seen slaves on horseback,
while princes go on foot like slaves.
Whoever digs a pit may fall into it;
whoever breaks through a wall may be
bitten by a snake.
Whoever quarries stones may be injured
by them;
whoever splits logs may be endan-
gered by them.
If the ax is dull
and its edge unsharpened,
more strength is needed
but skill will bring success.

If a snake bites before it is charmed,
there is no profit for the charmer.
Words from a wise man's mouth are gra-
cious,
but a fool is consumed by his own lips.
At the beginning his words are folly;
at the end they are wicked madness—
and the fool multiplies words.
No one knows what is coming—
who can tell him what will happen
after him?

A fool's work wearies him;
  he does not know the way to town.
Woe to you, O land whose king was a
    servant
  and whose princes feast in the morn-
    ing.
Blessed are you, O land whose king is of
    noble birth
  and whose princes eat at a proper
    time—
  for strength and not for drunkenness.

If a man is lazy, the rafters sag;
  if his hands are idle, the house leaks.

A feast is made for laughter,
  and wine makes life merry,
  but money is the answer for every-
    thing.

Do not revile the king even in your
    thoughts,
  or curse the rich in your bedroom,
because a bird of the air may carry your
    words,
  and a bird on the wing may report
    what you say.

Cast your bread upon the waters,
for after many days you will find it again.

Give portions to seven, yes to eight,
  for you do not know what disaster may
    come upon the land.

If clouds are full of water,
  they pour rain upon the earth.
Whether a tree falls to the south or to the
    north,
  in the place where it falls, there will it
    lie.
Whoever watches the wind will not plant;
  whoever looks at the clouds will not
    reap.
As you do not know the path of the wind,

or how the body is formed in a moth-
    er's womb,
so you cannot understand the work of
    God,
  the Maker of all things.

Sow your seed in the morning,
  and at evening let not your hands be
    idle,
for you do not know which will succeed,
  whether this or that,
  or whether both will do equally well.
                    —Ecclesiastes 9:13-11:6

"Eat your food with gladness" (9:7) Qoheleth has urged us, as he presented us with his literary sandwich (9:1-12). He now offers us much more varied fare, a delightful stew of traditional wisdom sayings spiced up by his own critical comments and fortified by his own observations and conclusions. Here we do not find a sparse, carefully layered structure but a wider sampling of loosely connected bits and pieces that wisdom has to offer, all thrown together in the same pot.

As before (7:1-8:1) Qoheleth gladly dishes out the words of the wise, but again he cannot resist commenting on the missing ingredients and the morsels his own observation would suggest we do not swallow.

The Thanks You Get! (9:13-16)

To test again wisdom's limits, Qoheleth introduces a story about a little city attacked by a powerful king. The bad news is that the Hebrew in which he tells the story is just ambiguous enough to allow us to interpret it in two distinctly different ways. The good news is that either interpretation works equally well. The difficulty comes in verse 15:

*Now there lived in that city a man poor
but wise, and he saved the city by his wisdom. But nobody remembered that poor
man.*

(9:15)

The NIV and RSV both tell us that the
poor man actually saved the city but that
soon everybody forgot about him. The
Hebrew would also allow as an equally
credible translation: "he *could have* saved
the city by his wisdom, but *nobody
thought of him*," and so they never bothered asking him.

In either case, Qoheleth tells this story
to voice once more his standard refrain
on wisdom: it has value, but only limited
value (2:13-14).

If you're a romantic, you'll want to go
with the NIV's translation in which
Qoheleth tells us that obviously wisdom
had value because it allowed even a poor
man to save a city (although he gives no
details on how). Unfortunately, this wise
action did not bring any lasting honor or
fame to the soon-forgotten hero.

If you're having a bad day and your
misery loves company, then you can take
the second translation. In this rendering
of the Hebrew, the man's wisdom went to
waste because his fellow city dwellers
simply overlooked him.

Qoheleth, then, is telling us that wisdom can do great things, but we cannot
always find a way to access it. It's something like forgetting where we put that
recipe box. We may have all the informa-
tion we need to make culinary history,
but it's macaroni and cheese again if we
can't find it. Possessing wisdom is no
guarantee that we can actually make use
of it.

Despite the negative outcome of the
story (in either case), Qoheleth concludes
that

*"Wisdom is better than strength." But the
poor man's wisdom is despised, and his
words are no longer heeded.*

(9:16)

Here again Qoheleth interrupts a traditional wisdom saying to show its limitation: Brain is better than brawn—*Yes, but*
only when it's used, and only for so long!

A Little Folly, A Lot of Grief (9:17-10:3)

Qoheleth continues to explore that
theme. The quiet, sensible words of the
wise outweigh the ear-shattering bluster
of even the most powerful fool (9:17).
Similarly, a wise plan outguns even the
most forceful weapons (9:18). *Yes, but*
one measly sin, one stupid move outweighs all that wisdom (9:18, 10:1)—just
as some dead flies ruin a whole jar of
ointment, or one fling destroys a brilliant
career, or one slip at the wheel wipes out
an entire busload of university seniors.

Despite such limitations, it's obvious
that wisdom is still better than folly: "The
heart of the wise inclines to the right, but
the heart of the fool to the left" (10:2).
Qoheleth is not making a political statement here. In ancient Oriental culture, as
in many cultures today, one always dif-
ferentiated between the left and right
hand. The right hand was put strictly to
"modest" use, like preparing food; the
left hand to "immodest" use, like tending
to *really* basic hygiene in a land where
water was precious and paper was used
only for writing. So Qoheleth simply
observes that all things being equal, wise
people more often than not lean toward
lofty pursuits while fools have their
minds in the gutter.

Even the way he goes about trying to
pursue his evil goals shows how mindless

and stupid the fool is: "even as he walks along the road, the fool lacks sense . . ." (10:3). The Hebrew says literally "lacks a heart." The ancients took the heart to be the seat of knowledge and wisdom. In our idiom we would simply say that the fool "shows he hasn't got a brain in his head."

Some Tips on Politics (10:4-7)

Maybe his mention of "the quiet words of the wise" (9:17) triggers in Qoheleth's mind another bit of advice he wants to share, even though it seems unrelated to what he has just observed.

If a ruler's anger rises against you, do not leave your post; calmness can lay great errors to rest.
(10:4)

Keep your cool when your superior loses his. And oh, yes . . . speaking of rulers reminds him of something else he wanted to tell us: rulers sometimes make really stupid mistakes. They put fools in high positions and bust the really qualified administrators back down to the mail room (10:5-7).

Not wise, Qoheleth warns—not wise to turn the pyramid on its head like that. Wisdom, practical experience, insight, skill— these things are needed so desperately in sensitive leadership positions. That holds true for government as well as any other area of life. What happens to churches when our brightest and best are no longer going to the seminaries or warming the chairs in the council room? Call him conservative, but Qoheleth shudders. Too many communities have been devastated by incompetent leadership. We can fashion even democracy into an idol that demands too high a sacrifice. It can make us give up well-equipped, skilled, experienced leadership

for the sake of having our own biased, uneducated say.

Minimizing the Risk (10:8-11)

Qoheleth throws into the pot another good reason for valuing practical wisdom: it minimizes the damage our work may cause us. It's a sad fact of life that our efforts, which are supposed to improve our situation, can take a nasty turn and do just the opposite.

Whoever digs a pit may fall into it; whoever breaks through a wall may be bitten by a snake. Whoever quarries stones may be injured by them; whoever splits logs may be endangered by them.
(10:8-9)

But using your head can help you to prevent that. Take the last example. Split logs with a dull ax, and you need to use more raw muscle (10:10). But the more power you use, the less control you have, and the more easily you could get hurt by the rebounding blade or the flying chunks of wood. Better to be wise and hone that ax head to a fine sharp edge. That'll bring success.

Still not convinced that knowing how to do the job right is more important than brute force? "If a snake bites before it is charmed, there is no profit for the charmer" (10:11). *No kidding!* The fact that nobody will pay a cent to watch him writhe in agony is the least of his worries! Without the proper skill, it makes no difference how much weight he can bench press or how impressive his pects. He's dead.

Of Empty Barrels (10:12-15)

Qoheleth continues his stream-of-consciousness investigation into the relative merits of practical wisdom. The quiet (9:17), gracious words of the wise build up their reputations, while the babble of fools causes theirs to self-destruct (10:12). They even advertise their stupidity by a constant stream of worthless chatter (10:14a) that's nothing but silliness from beginning to end (10:13). The empty barrel makes the most noise.

Yes, but "No one knows what is coming—who can tell him what will happen after him?" (10:14b). Fools can't. But the wise can't either. So they're in the same boat after all.

To be sure, but at least the wise know when to shut up! It's better to remain silent and be thought wise than to speak and be shown to be a fool.

So being wise in what we say helps us build a good reputation. And that has real, although temporary (9:13-16), benefit. The same holds true for our work. Real craftsmanship minimizes risk (10:10) and gives us enjoyment in a job well done. But "A fool's work wearies him; he does not know the way to town" (10:15). Bumblers stupid enough not to know the way home certainly cannot find their way around the workplace either. No wonder work "drives them nuts!"

According to the "Peter Principle," many people in large corporations or in the civil service get promoted to their own level of incompetence. Because they're doing such a good job, the company continues to promote them. But they finally reach a point at which they have overreached their limits: they've been promoted to a job they are not equipped to handle. And they are stuck there. Nobody wants to risk a major blowup by putting them back where they belong. So there they hang: unproductive, unhappy, and left to rot.

The same holds true for so many small business operators who take a shot at the big leagues. High leveraging swallows up in a day what it took them a lifetime to build.

How sad! Overreaching ourselves like that makes our work burdensome in ways that God never intended. God gave us work to do to make us happy and talents to allow us to do that work. But our Maker never asks us to use talents we don't have. Wise people play to their strong suit. When they find themselves pushed into a position outside of their area of competence or beyond their level of skill, they look for more suitable work before it's too late—before the weariness caused by their ignorance and lack of skill causes them to fall apart.

Flotsam (10:16-20)

Wanting to show us more of the garden's mysteries, Qoheleth pulls us from here to there. In our wandering, some unconnected bits and pieces drift through our awareness.

Look! Over there! How sad! "Woe to you, O land, when your king is a child, and your princes feast in the morning!" (10:16 RSV) Unlike the "poor but wise youth" of chapter 4:13, this lummox is a genuine small fry. He's so young and foolish that he and his buddies use their position of responsibility only to fill their own bellies and leave the ship of state rudderless. Better stuff over there, Qoheleth points out:

Happy are you, O land, when your king is the son of free men, and your princes feast at the proper time, for strength, and not for drunkenness!

(10:17 RSV)

Do we recognize some of the people Qoheleth talks about here? Doesn't this garden seem strangely familiar? Looks suspiciously like the one on Capitol Hill—pork barrel, "watering hole," and all!

No time to dawdle, Qoheleth pushes us on. What applies to heads of state applies equally well to the common Joe: "If a man is lazy, the rafters sag; if his hands are idle, the house leaks" (10:18). Aha, there's more of the Calvinist in him then he dared to admit in chapter 4:6! And the next bit of wisdom he shows us seems to clinch that suspicion:

A feast is made for laughter, and wine makes life merry, but money is the answer for everything.

(10:19)

We know him too well not to notice that he has his tongue firmly in his cheek. He has taught us too much about the poverty of being money-hungry (5:10), the painful sting riches carry with them (5:13), and the fleeting value of the dollar (5:15). Using good Hebrew hyperbole here, he overstates the case: money answers *everything*. Everything? Well . . . everything *under the sun*—for *now* at least. You won't feast without it, you know! You can't buy wine with buttons. Money can't buy happiness, but it sure helps! You won't be happy for long without it. Before you stock that fridge and that wine rack, be sure you've stocked your bank account. Prudent stewardship requires no less.

Before taking us to the beach (11:1), Qoheleth gives us one more quick peek at the roses in wisdom's garden. Their sharp thorns signal a suitably stern warning:

Do not revile the king even in your thoughts, or curse the rich in your bedroom, because a bird of the air may carry your words, and a bird on the wing may report what you say.

(10:20)

Sound advice: one slip of the tongue, one tiny breach of confidentiality, one misplaced insult, and we're ruined. Once the cat is out of the bag, nothing can get it back in there. So don't even *think* of saying something stupid that could get back to you. Such things have a strange way of doing just that.

Risk It! (11:1-6)

In due time Qoheleth will take us up to the top of the hill from which can gain one last comprehensive view of the whole garden. But before doing that he needs to clear up a possible misunderstanding we might have gained from his previous discussion. So he takes us to the seashore first.

Earlier Qoheleth taught us:

The race is not to the swift or the battle to the strong, nor does food come to the wise or wealth to the brilliant or favor to the learned; but time and chance happen to them all.

(9:11)

That observation could paralyze us. Why try anything at all if our efforts may not get us anywhere? If you can't win anyway, why roll the dice?

Qoheleth reminds us that his aim is to alert us to the fact that life offers us no guarantees. The world and the One who controls it are much more complex than we can imagine. So counting on our own efforts to achieve anything lasting will sooner or later fail. In this fallen creation

there's no such thing as a sure thing,
Qoheleth observes.

But does that mean we should not
work? Does it mean we should not try to
get somewhere? Should we just rot in
bed?

Of course not! Qoheleth chides. That's
taking things from one idolatrous
extreme to the other: it's called fatalism.
He points to the ships out on the sea, their
bellies stuffed with precious cargo. See
how the merchants take such incredible
risks! Their daily bread and butter floats
only one skinny boat hull out of reach of
the briny deep and certain bankruptcy.
But they take the risk. Good for them!

"Cast *your* bread upon the waters, for
after many days you will find it again"
(11:1). As the merchants prove: Nothing
ventured, nothing gained.

Commerce is one way we can invest.
Who knows? God might allow the odds
to go in our favor. Another way is gen-
erosity:

Give portions to seven, yes to eight, for
you do not know what disaster may come
upon the land.
(11:2)

Like Jesus did in the parable of the
unjust steward (Luke 16:1f), Qoheleth
tells us to spread the wealth around while
we have it, so that we'll have friends to
help us out when our bad times come—as
they inevitably will (9:12).

A third example of the wisdom of prudent risk-taking that Qoheleth cites is that
of a farmer seeding the crop. A farmer
takes a calculated gamble that the high
investment and hard work will ultimately
pay off in a profitable harvest. But who
knows? The sky might not rain, or it
might rain too much (11:3a), or the wind
might blow in from the wrong direction.

In Palestine, if the wind knocks trees
over in a southward direction, then it's a
fresh, invigorating, moisture-laden
northerly. But if the tree falls to the north,
then the wind blows in from the south,
across hundreds of miles of bone-dry
desert (11:3b). The arid, scorching heat
will ruin the crop for sure.

We have no control over the weather.
If we wait for optimum conditions, then
we'll never get the seed in. And we'll get
no crop out. We have no choice but to
take the risk (11:4), hope for the best, and
leave the results in God's hands. In all
our risk-taking we do well to follow the
prairie farmers' advice: first plant, *then*
complain.

We know so little, Qoheleth reminds
us:

As you do not know the path of the wind,
or how the body is formed in a mother's
womb, so you cannot understand the
work of God, the Maker of all things.
(11:5)

The Hebrew in this passage can also
be translated:

As you do not know how the spirit comes
to the bones in the womb of a woman
with child, so you do not know the work
of God who makes everything.
(11:5 RSV)

In either case, Qoheleth reminds us
how limited our wisdom is, and how little
we understand of what God is doing.
Why does our Creator tear mountains
apart in violent volcanic eruptions? How
does our Sovereign Lord build the
typhoons, droughts, earthquakes, and tor-
nadoes that devastate the earth? Who
knows? We do not even know how God
made us!

But our ignorance does not have to paralyze us:

Sow your seed in the morning, and at evening let not your hands be idle, for you do not know which will succeed, whether this or that, or whether both will do equally well.

(11:6)

As much as we would like to, we cannot control the world so well that we can guarantee success. Our lifelong dependency on God keeps us living every day in our Father's will. Even Jesus, God's own Son, lived out of that creaturely dependency. Even *his* work did not always meet with success; quite the contrary. Faced with a violently stubborn people who rejected his Word wholesale, Jesus reached back to the farmer's wisdom: "A farmer went out to sow his seed . . ." (Matt. 13:3).

Jesus knew he could leave the harvest in his Father's hands. Despite the many failures, the Word he delivered would take root in the hearts of many. They would bring about a bumper crop—not the "normal" windfall crop of an eightfold increase, but "a hundred, sixty or thirty times what was sown" (Matt. 13:8). He knew there would be a rich harvest—because he knew his Father.

Like Jesus, like wise Qoheleth, and like every farmer, we too must keep our eye on the harvest.

An old Jewish tale tells of a grain farmer who comes to heaven's gate with a big chip on his shoulder. He asks to see Top Management and proceeds to pour out his complaint. "Sixty years I prayed and prayed for a good crop so I could scratch out a decent living for my family. Sixty years all I got was weeds, weeds, and more weeds. I begged, I pleaded, I cried, I humbled myself—but nothing. To be honest with you I'm pretty disappointed; if I may be so bold as to say."

Came the reply: "Yes, yes, I can certainly see why you're so disappointed. Sixty years is a long time to sit and wait . . . but together with your earnest prayer you *could* have tried to sow some grain."

CHAPTER ELEVEN

When You're Young

Light is sweet,
  and it pleases the eyes to see
    the sun.

However many years a man may live,
  let him enjoy them all.
But let him remember the days of dark-
    ness,
  for they will be many.
  Everything to come is meaningless.

Be happy, young man, while you are
    young,
  and let your heart give you joy in the
    days of your youth.
Follow the ways of your heart
  and whatever your eyes see,
but know that for all these things
  God will bring you to judgment.
So then, banish anxiety from your heart
  and cast off the troubles of your body,
  for youth and vigor are meaningless.

Remember your Creator
in the days of your youth,
before the days of trouble come
  and the years approach when you will
    say,
  "I find no pleasure in them"—
before the sun and the light
  and the moon and the stars grow dark,

and the clouds return after the
    rain;
  when the keepers of the house
    tremble,
  and the strong men stoop,
when the grinders cease because they are
    few,
  and those looking through the win-
    dows grow dim;
when the doors to the street are closed
  and the sound of grinding fades;
when men rise up at the sound of birds,
  but all their songs grow faint;
when men are afraid of heights
  and of dangers in the streets;
when the almond tree blossoms
  and the grasshopper drags himself
    along
  and desire no longer is stirred.
Then man goes to his eternal home
  and mourners go about the streets.

Remember him—before the silver cord is
    severed,
  or the golden bowl is broken;
before the pitcher is shattered at the
    spring,
  or the wheel broken at the well,
and the dust returns to the ground it
    came from,

and the spirit returns to God who gave it.

"Meaningless! Meaningless!" says the Teacher.
"Everything is meaningless!"
—*Ecclesiastes 11:7-12:8*

Light is sweet, and it pleases the eyes to see the sun. However many years a man may live, let him enjoy them all. But let him remember the days of darkness, for they will be many. Everything to come is meaningless.

(11:7-8)

Televisions have a "contrast" knob that allows us to choose the amount of variation we want between the colors and shades that create the images on our screen. On a black-and-white set, the contrast knob controls the relative difference between the blacks, the whites, and the mediating grays. Turn the contrast way down, and all the features of the image dissolve into a single pool of nothingness. But when we turn the knob up, the blacks become blacker and the whites whiter, and the picture pops clearly into view. The higher we set the contrast, the more clearly defined the image becomes.

That's exactly what Qoheleth wants to do for us one last time, before he signs off. He wants to make us see how good and beautiful and precious life is. So he paints the contrast as clearly as he can. He places the beauty of life squarely up against the backdrop of the darkness that one day awaits us: the gloom of old age sliding us all too soon into inevitable death. "Better to go to a house of mourning than to go to a house of feasting," (7:2) he has taught us. So in our mind's eye, that's exactly where he's taking us next.

The Dark Days Will Come (11:7-8)

Qoheleth begins our field trip by advising us not to turn the "contrast" button all the way down. If we try vainly to screen out the darkness, we will not be able to fully appreciate the light either:

We naturally wish to avoid looking at the dark days ahead because we love the light of life. And that light is good, Qoheleth agrees. Enjoy it while you can. But show some courage and look at the darkness too. Dare to visualize yourself in the extended care bed and even in your coffin. Taking a look at those realities now will constantly remind you how precious your health and strength really are while you have them, spurring you on to make the most of your life.

Strangely enough it's only when old age makes our eyes go dim that we gain the clearest vision of life as a whole. When senior citizens are asked what they would do differently if they could do it all over again, their response invariably goes something like this: "I'd do it just about the way I did it the first time. But I would take a lot more time to smell the roses, to enjoy my kids when I still had 'em with me, and to do the fun things I denied myself in trying to get ahead."

In life, as on a cross-country tour or a wilderness hiking trip, the real fun is in getting there. But especially when we're young, our restless hearts keep raising that familiar whine: "Aren't we there yet!?"

Go for It with Your God! (11:9-10)

Qoheleth directs himself very specifically to the young:

Be happy, young man, while you are young, and let your heart give you joy in

*the days of your youth. Follow the ways
of your heart and whatever your eyes see.*
                                        (11:9a)

"*Carpe diem,*" Qoheleth urges, "seize
the day!" Today God has given you
health and strength and vigor and dreams.
Go for it! Don't let those jaded old
geezers stop you from having a really
good time. Enjoy your youth while you
still can. Chase your dreams and ambitions with all you've got. Set the world
on its ear—who says it can't be done?
Experience it all. Live it up!

Okay, teacher . . . so where's the
catch? We know it's coming, so go ahead
and lay it on us: ". . . but know that for all
these things God will bring you to judgment (11:9b)."

See, we knew it! Here comes the big
but: but do your homework or God will
get you for not doing your best; *but* clean
up your room and take that shower
because cleanliness is next to godliness;
but don't think life's just a picnic because
God will get mad if you don't fulfill all
your responsibilities. . . .

On the contrary, Qoheleth insists: "so
then, banish anxiety from your heart and
cast off the troubles of your body . . ."
(11:10a).

Hold on a second. We've heard the
speech so often about how God is going
to judge everything we do. It always ends
with a big lecture about being responsible
and doing all our duties, blah, blah, blah.
How can Qoheleth tell us that God's
judgment should somehow make us care-
free? We've never heard the speech end
that way before.

Qoheleth raises the issue of God's
judgment precisely because he wants to
throw gasoline, not cold water, on youthful enthusiasm. God's judgment is not the
big catch, but the big energizer. It fills

our lives with importance and meaning
and purpose despite the fact that nothing
we set out to do will accomplish anything
lasting. It matters to God what we do.
Nobody else may care that we finally
managed to ride that two-wheeler, but
God does! Our friends don't give us a
standing ovation every time we buckle
down and pass another exam, but God
rejoices! His caring elevates to a higher
level our excitement at meeting life's
challenges and celebrating life's genuine
delight. We have a Friend who shows a
whole lot more interest than our parents,
our classmates, or anybody else.

"God has already approved what you
do!" (9:7 RSV) Qoheleth has told us.
When we appear before God on judgment
day he's not going to ask us: "Did you
mow the lawn? And did you wash behind
your ears?" God's real concern is that we
make our lives into something for which
we, and those around us, can genuinely
be thankful (Matt. 5:16; 1 Thess. 5:18).

Fear of the Bench?

We can be so schizophrenic in our
faith. On the one hand we confess that in
Jesus all our sins and shortcomings are
washed away and all his good works are
credited to our account. On the other
hand we worry about facing God, scared
stiff that when our Lord opens the Big
Book, he'll angrily shake his head and
stare down his holy nose at us.

It won't be like that. Judgment Day
will bring those of us who are in Christ to
a joyful reunion. We'll square accounts
with those who tripped up God's children
(Matt. 18:6-7; Matt. 25:45-46). How
could it be any different when our own
lawyer is the Judge? (Matt. 25:31).
Children of God who love him and know
they are loved by him have no more fear
of God's judgment. The apostle John tells

us: "Love is made complete among us so that we will have confidence on the day of judgment, because in this world we are like him. There is no fear in love. But perfect love drives out fear . . ." (1 John 4:17-18).

Therefore Paul also constantly reminds us to rejoice. The real badge of a Christian is not suffering or doing one's duty. Pagans also do those things. What really makes us stand out is our inextinguishable joy—even during hard times. That celebration of life in Christ makes us Good News to a hurting world that still tries to bear sin's heavy burden on its own shoulders.

So drop that yoke, Qoheleth advises, ". . . for youth and vigor are meaningless" (11:10b).

The less we have of something, the more precious and valuable we deem it. So treasure your childhood while you can, Qoheleth urges, before you let it slip away without enjoying it to the full.

And grown-ups, give those kids a break! The young 'uns will carry the responsibilities and burdens of life soon enough. Give them some space. Help them make the most of the time when everything is still fresh and new and exciting. God invites us to be as Christ to them:

I praise you, Father, Lord of heaven and earth, because you have hidden these things from the wise and learned, and revealed them to little children. Yes, Father for this was your good pleasure . . . Come to me all you who are weary and burdened, and I will give you rest. Take my yoke upon you and learn from me, for I am gentle and humble in heart, and you will find rest for your souls. For my yoke is easy and my burden is light.
—Matthew 11:28-30

The Approaching Darkness (12:1)

Qoheleth sums it up: "Remember your Creator in the days of your youth, before the days of trouble come and the years approach when you will say, 'I find no pleasure in them'" (12:1).

Remembering God means walking with him and letting him guide us through life. It means letting him teach us what is wise and what leads to real joy. God made us. Walking in our Maker's ways maximizes our chances of being happy while we still have the chance. Only in that way can we take up God's challenge to accept responsibility for our own happiness "before the days of trouble come" (12:1).

Not even one out of five VCR owners knows how to properly set one up to fill one of its most useful functions: to tape a television show when they're not around. Why? Because they have never bothered reading the manual that the factory supplies with the product. Silly really. It may be a chore, but a half hour of mental effort can yield such rich rewards.

The same is true for human beings. Our Creator issued an instruction manual for us too: the invigorating, sweet, and joy-bearing law (Ps.19:7-11). God's intent is not to burden us with endless restrictions and obligations. He only wants to show us how, in a broken world, we can still maximize our happiness and live up to our fullest potential.

To stress how urgently and passionately our Creator wants young people to enjoy life with their God while they still have their youthful vigor and their faculties, Qoheleth paints a marvelously striking picture of what old age will bring. He throws the images around rather freely and loosely, so we must not try to force an overly rigorous, airtight pattern of interpretation on them. What we do find are some extended metaphors running through his keenly perceptive description, all relating in a playful way to the foibles of old age.

Age-old Deficits (12:2-5)

In verses 2-4 he takes us to a decrepit old mansion in which the doddering old inhabitants weather one more major storm. The various elements of the disintegrating wreck neatly correspond to the various parts of the body that wear out when old age finally gets the better of us.

"Remember your Creator . . . before the sun and the light and the moon and the stars grow dark, and the clouds return after the rain . . ." (12:2). The storm clouds gather. The light grows dim as cataracts and glaucoma bring on failing eyesight. Things won't get better either. In younger years we could still expect recovery; the blue skies would return after the winter rains. But now we weather one storm after another.

". . . When the keepers of the house tremble" (12:3a). The butler and the gardener now turn milk to butter simply by holding it in their hands. They still keep the place going, but just barely. This image describes what our hands will be like. They may still keep us shaved and fed, but not without leaving a few nasty cuts on our face and a spoonful or two of yesterday's dinner on our shirt.

". . . And the strong men stoop" (12:3b). When they actually manage to stand up, the security guard and the maintenance man now go through life permanently examining their (probably mismatched) socks; our legs won't let us stand straight anymore; bad knees, you know!

". . . When the grinders cease because they are few" (12:3c). The old women who would grind the grain to bake bread have all but gone; without our choppers, steak has to make way for oatmeal and soup.

". . . And those looking through the windows grow dim" (12:3d). The ladies still peer out of the windows through the lattice. That way they can see what is going on in the street without immodestly allowing passers-by to see them in return. But now the growing darkness of the storm won't let them catch the juicy details anymore of who is walking with whom, or spying out what Martha's taking home from the market in that oversized basket. Compare that to eyes now grown old. They won't let us read anymore, so mostly we just sit and recollect, staring at nothing more than the memories themselves now long-since faded.

". . . When the doors to the street are closed and the sound of grinding fades" (12:4a, b). The Hebrew mentions double doors here, the ones one finds only in palaces, mansions, or city gates. The storm dictates their closure, shutting out the street sounds, or at least muffling them. "It isn't that we can't hear anymore. It's just that those young whippersnappers today have not been taught to speak clearly: they rattle on so fast without properly enunciating. Why, in the old days we were taught how to speak clearly, by cracky . . . now, what was I saying?"

Qoheleth presses on, leaving the image of the old house behind but continuing to describe the deficits of old age.

". . . When men rise up at the sound of birds, but all their songs grow faint" (12:4c, d). We cannot sleep soundly anymore; any peep will startle us and wake

us up. But when we listen for the birds' songs, we can barely hear them anymore.

"... *When men are afraid of heights and of dangers in the streets*" *(12:5a, b)*. A curb may as well be a 100-meter gorge, and a loose paving stone a rock slide. Our fears of those things now keep us practically under house arrest.

"... *When the almond tree blossoms*" *(12:5c)*. Almond tree blossoms turn white, just like our hair would have, if we still had any left.

"... *And the grasshopper drags himself along*" *(12:5d)*. We do the same slow, crazy, strained walk as an overstuffed grasshopper dragging its bloated belly.

"... *And desire no longer is stirred* *(12:5e)*. The Hebrew literally reads "... and the caperberry fails." The seeds of the caperberry bush were used to stimulate the appetite. But appetizers just can't interest us in food anymore.

And when these things happen, "*Then man goes to his eternal home and mourners go about the streets*" *(12:5f, g)*. After the light fails at dusk, night falls in dead earnest.

Then . . . the End (12:6-8)

Like sunset in the tropics, death can steal the light of life so quickly it catches us completely off guard. Qoheleth brings in two new images to show how suddenly and finally death takes us out of the picture, affording us no time to get reacquainted with our Creator if we have not already done so:

Remember him—before the silver cord is severed, or the golden bowl is broken; before the pitcher is shattered at the spring, or the wheel broken at the well. . . .
(12:6)

In the first image a beautiful, golden oil lamp hangs from the wall suspended by a silver chain. It could have hung there gracefully giving its light for decades. But all of a sudden the chain snaps, and BANG! the lamp crashes to the floor, its light permanently extinguished.

In the second image, life-giving water trickles uselessly away from the shards of a busted water jug. Worse, the water cannot be replenished because the wheel used to haul it up is also broken. What is gone is gone for good.

Qoheleth leaves metaphor behind and speaks plainly:

and the dust returns to the ground it came from, and the spirit returns to God who gave it.
(12:7)

Here he depicts graphically how death reverses the process by which God breathed us into being (Gen. 2:7). God gave us our life-breath. Now he it takes it back. All that we were, are, or could be, is now dumped into the grave: dust to dust. Our hopes, our dreams, our achievements, our failures, our joys, our sorrows, our laughter, and our tears all disappear with us down that hole—as if we'd never even existed.

Since 1:1 forms an introduction and 12:9-14 a postlude, Qoheleth's own message ends exactly where it began (1:2):

"Meaningless! Meaningless!" says the Teacher. "Everything is meaningless!"
(12:8)

Like his literary sandwich in Chapter 9, Qoheleth frames his entire discourse with the harsh fact of our inability and insignificance. But like a fancy clubhouse triple-decker, he stacks layer upon layer

of good stuff to chew on in between
(2:24-26; 3:12-14, 22; 5:18-20; 8:15; 9:7-
9; 11:9, 10).

Disregard the inside, and Qoheleth
turns into nothing more than another
cynic unburdening his tormented soul
because his misery craves company. Take
away the outside frame, and we turn him
into just another jet-setting playboy. To
prevent such misunderstanding, he carefully structures his message so we will
wisely make our enjoyment of these God-
breathed words a truly nourishing feast.

With Childlike Abandon

Coming inside from the backyard to
take a bath is torture enough. But going
to sleep in a strange bed and a strange
room scares the youngsters to death. The
icy darkness threatens them with horrify-
ing monsters and poisonous snakes. Is
that really a gloved hand reaching out of
the closet? Is that awful noise some
hideous creature growling at them from
under the bed?

How relieved and peacefully they
drift off to sleep when Grandpa sits with
them and tells them a story: "Once upon
a time, long ago, when it was still dark, a
lady called Mary went to the tomb and
saw that the stone had been removed. . . ."

CHAPTER TWELVE

The Bottom Line Resolved

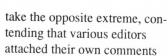

Not only was the Teacher wise, but also he imparted knowledge to the people. He pondered and searched out and set in order many proverbs. The Teacher searched to find just the right words, and what he wrote was upright and true.

The words of the wise are like goads, their collected sayings like firmly embedded nails—given by one Shepherd. Be warned, my son, of anything in addition to them.

Of making many books there is no end, and much study wearies the body.

Now all has been heard;
 here is the conclusion of the matter:
Fear God and keep his commandments,
 for this is the whole duty of man.
For God will bring every deed into judgment,
 including every hidden thing,
 whether it is good or evil.
 —Ecclesiastes 12:9-14

Commentators wage a heated debate over who added the appendix to Ecclesiastes (12:9-14). Some vigorously defend the proposition that Qoheleth penned these words, reverting to speaking of himself in the third person. Others take the opposite extreme, contending that various editors attached their own comments piecemeal. They imagine that a well-wishing student of Qoheleth might have appended much of verses 9-11 because he wanted to stick up for his mentor's reputation. A second editor, more critical than the first, added parts of verses 12-14, trying to smooth out the rough spots where he thought the book collided with traditional orthodoxy. Subsequent editors then added their own glosses, trying to smooth out the ending to best fit their own purposes. Most commentators accept the mediating opinion that the whole appendix was attached by a single editor who not only understood the Teacher's message thoroughly, but knew him personally as well (12:9).

The issue should not really matter too much to us, since it is the text we have before us in its present form that we accept as the canonical, unfailing Word of God (12:11). Whether it comes from one pen or from three or more, it is this final edition that we accept as Spirit-inspired truth. Its authority does not rest on who (re)wrote it but Who inspired it. Although we may play around with different theories concerning the Bible's formation, we should ultimately accept, interpret, leave, and live God's Word "as is."

A Glimpse at the Author (12:9-10)

Whoever wrote these words knew Qoheleth personally. If he was not Qoheleth himself, he may have been an associate or a student of the Teacher. Because he addresses us as "my son" (12:12), we may assume that he also was a teacher. And he must have respected Qoheleth a great deal, because he says some very kind things about him:

Not only was the Teacher wise, but also he imparted knowledge to the people.
(12:9a)

That the Teacher was wise seems plain enough. Intelligent chap! But wisdom involves more than simple head knowledge or intellectual brilliance. "Wisdom" in the biblical sense carries with it the idea of solid, practical insight into everyday living. It's characteristics are skill, know-how, and the ability to act intelligently where the rubber hits the road. No ivory-tower theoretician, this Qoheleth—he was a real down-to-earth wise guy.

Equally to Qoheleth's credit, he taught the common people. He did not just seek to satisfy his own intellectual curiosity or to rub elbows exclusively with fellow academics. He cared enough about Baruch the baker to share the results of his learning with him.

Qoheleth achieved what should be every Christian scholar's goal: he made a meaningful contribution not only to his own discipline but to the wider Christian community as well. Truly brilliant scholarship informs daily living. If scholars cannot convey the fruits of their research plainly enough for flower growers and homemakers to understand, then maybe they have not mastered their subject well enough.

Not that such "popularizing" is always easy. Qoheleth sweated blood over that part of his task:

He pondered and searched out and set in order many proverbs. The Teacher searched to find just the right words, and what he wrote was upright and true.
(12:9b-10)

Unfortunately, our English translation loses much of the vividness of the Hebrew. The editor here consistently employs Hebrew verb forms that intensify their meanings. Qoheleth pondered like crazy. He searched and searched. He spared no effort to set his words in precisely the right order. He pored over them to get them just so.

Quiet! Author at Work (12:9)

Qoheleth's editor here gives us some unique insights into the Teacher's methodology.

He pondered proverbs—literally, he "weighed" them (12:9). He tried hard to strike the proper balance (see for example 9:13-18). Ever buy cheese in a store where they still use an old-fashioned balancing scale? Constant adjustments must be made, first to one side then to the other; adding this here, that there, until the scale is in perfect balance. That is no mean feat with cheese, but it's a thousand times harder with wisdom sayings!

Second, Qoheleth "studied" (RSV), "searched out" (NIV) proverbs. In his apocryphal book, Ben Sira uses that same word in the sense of "compose" (Sir. 44:5). Qoheleth not only tried to balance the varying lines of advice he found in existing proverbs, but he also used his own keen observations to mold new ones.

Third, he "arrang[ed]" them (RSV), "set [them] in order" (NIV). He assembled them into literary units that would give wider and more comprehensive insight. By carefully relating them, he crafted a whole that is bigger than the sum of its parts. Here we are cautioned to read the book not as just a grab bag of disconnected bits of wit. The way Qoheleth has organized his material makes sense. We're urged to appreciate the interrelationships and the unity of the Teacher's underlying message.

Pleasant Words (12:10)

Our editor tells us that "The Teacher searched to find just the right words" (12:10). The Hebrew literally has "words of delight." We can readily agree that "what he wrote was upright and true" (12:10)—but can we really call these "delightful" words?

"Utterly meaningless! Everything is meaningless."
(1:2)

Better to go to a house of mourning than a house of feasting.
(7:2)

There is not a righteous man on earth who does what is right and never sins.
(7:20)

This is the evil in everything that happens under the sun: The same destiny overtakes all.
(9:3)

These words may be true, but only a really twisted masochist would find them "delightful!"

Really? There are at least three ways in which Qoheleth's words are precisely that.

First, like the painting *Guernica*, in which Pablo Picasso depicts the cruel horror of the Nazi bombing of a tiny Spanish village, Qoheleth's work is not pretty or nice; but it's artistically and aesthetically very pleasing indeed. Like any masterpiece, the book of Ecclesiastes grasps the very essence of truth and beautifully stabs it into our hearts. Its wonderful compression and intensity of meaning forever changes our vision of the world. After experiencing this book, we'll never see or be the same.

Second, Qoheleth's words are delightful because they are intellectually crisp and clean. How students bless professors who do not need to drone on for hour after boring hour, but who convey a wealth of learning in a few well-chosen paragraphs. How gratefully the wider community listens when such a professor can leave the mystifying jargon and the dry-as-dust lecture notes in the study and just tell it like it is in plain Hebrew (English?). That may give academically fussy translators headaches, but it sure delights "the people" (12:9).

Third, Qoheleth's words are a delight in a much more profound way. He dares to "name the demon." Especially at times when we really hurt, when we're really depressed and despondent, the last thing we want to receive is cheap comfort. When we suddenly lose our job less than a decade away from retirement, we do not need to hear, "Hey, cheer up, pal— now you can take a really long vacation." When a relationship crumbles, we don't want to hear, "There's plenty more fish in the sea." At our husband's funeral we do not need to hear, "You can be glad he didn't suffer as much as Uncle Charlie, dear."

Not even the many resurrection texts our pastor or friends quote from the New Testament help us very much when a loved one suddenly dies. Nicholas Wolterstorff gives his perspective on this in *Lament For a Son*, a book in which he reflects on the accidental death of his son Eric:

> Elements of the gospel which I had always thought would console me did not. They did something else, something important, but not that. It did not console me to be reminded of the hope of resurrection. If I had forgotten that hope, then it would indeed have brought light into my life to be reminded of it. But I did not think of death as a bottomless pit. I did not grieve as one who has no hope. Yet Eric is gone, *here* and *now* he is gone; *now* I cannot talk with him, *now* I cannot see him, *now* I cannot hug him, *now* I cannot hear of his plans for the future. *That* is my sorrow. A friend said, "Remember, he's in good hands." I was deeply moved. But that reality does not put Eric back in my hands now. That's my grief. For that grief what consolation can there be other than having him back?
> —Lament For A Son, *p. 31*

The Teacher's words aren't like those of would-be consolers. He dares to walk beside us and feel our pain. He faces life's cruelty head-on and gives us the tools to truly express what we feel. In that way his words are delightful. They're RIGHT ON! Like a greater Teacher did in time's fullness, Qoheleth helps us bear our cross—not by soft-soaping our suffering, but by deeply living into our situation and helping us through it. He leads us on to the soul-warming embrace of the only Source of our abiding comfort in life and in death.

Goading Us On (12:11)

This bittersweet flavor of Qoheleth's words reminds the editor of a fitting proverb:

The words of the wise are like goads,
their collected sayings like firmly embedded nails—given by one Shepherd.
(12:11)

Ox goads were pre-twentieth-century cattle prods. They "encouraged" the animals to go where they were supposed to go. Using this nail-studded stick was unpleasant for the farmer and even more so for the animals. But the goads were necessary to bring the animals to the intended destination. Similarly, the wise words of Qoheleth may hurt at times, but they bring us back to God. Thereby we recognize in them the voice of "one Shepherd."

Many people invented and recorded wisdom sayings—Qoheleth included. But their many voices blend into one: the voice of God.

Unless we recognize this fact, we have not taken their words seriously enough. Howard Van Till expresses it well in "Taking the Bible Seriously," Chapter 1 of *The Fourth Day*:

> The Bible is the "Word" of God, not the "words" of God. The Bible did not drop from the sky by an act of divine magic. God did not circumvent human means of writing, editing, and assembling the body of legal, historical, and literary documents that constitute the Bible. Yet, while the words of the

Bible were produced by human writers, the Bible as an organic whole functions as God's Word, holy Scripture.

—*The Fourth Day, p. 5*

In the fullness of time Jesus revealed: "I am the Good Shepherd. The Good Shepherd lays down his life for his sheep . . . I have other sheep . . . I must bring them also. They too will listen to my voice, and there shall be one flock and one Shepherd."

—*John 10:11, 16 (author's translation)*

Beware the Student's Craft (12:12)

At times the voices do not blend but rather contradict that of the Shepherd. Then the sheep must discriminate, because many wolves go about in shepherd's clothing trying to mimic his voice:

"Be warned, my son, of anything in addition to them. Of making many books there is no end, and much study wearies the body."

(12:12)

Our idle speculation often causes much mischief. In Qoheleth's day, wrangling over genealogical records and the finer points of law brought grief to thousands. In our own time, many people have burned their furniture because they naively believed people who boasted that they had figured out exactly when Jesus would return. Such so-called biblical "experts" present us with road map after road map of how, when, and where God will bring the loose ends of history back together. They chop the Bible into jigsaw puzzle pieces that they string together into whatever conceivable pattern suits them.

They at least get some royalties for their efforts. All their readers get out of it is a chance to scratch their heads and wonder where all these imaginative but contradictory voices really leave them. In all their hard studying they no longer hear the clear sound of their Shepherd.

So that we will study wisely, we can draw at least two further cautions from the editor's warning in 12:12.

The first is wonderfully put forward by Derek Kidner, who in his commentary *The Message of Ecclesiastes* quotes C.S. Lewis in this context. Kidner observes, "We grow addicted to research itself, in love with our hard questions. An answer would spoil everything." He then quotes a passage from *The Great Divorce*, where Lewis tells how the White Spirit invites such a chronic researcher to enter heaven:

"I can promise you . . . no scope for your talents: only forgiveness for having perverted them. No atmosphere of inquiry, for I will bring you not to the land of questions but of answers, and you shall see the face of God."

"Ah, but we must all interpret those beautiful words in our own way! For me there is no such thing as a final answer. The free wind of inquiry must always continue to blow through the mind, must it not?"

"Listen!" said the White Spirit. "Once you were a child. Once you knew what inquiry was for. There was a time when you asked questions because you wanted answers, and were glad when you had found them. Become that child again: even now."

"Ah, but when I became a man I put away childish things."

Kidner goes on to summarize the result:

"No argument, no appeal will avail against this infinite elasticity. The encounter, already fruitless, ends with the gentle sophist's remembering an appointment, making his apologies, and hurrying off to his discussion group in hell."
—The Message of Ecclesiastes, *p. 106*

May God give us Christian scholars who are not childish but who, even at the pinnacle of their success, remain ever childlike by humbly following where Jesus leads them.

The second caution in the editor's warning suggests that studying hard may provide us with nothing more than a headache. Not only *that* we study but *what* we study matters. Choosing wisely what we read and what we write is as important for our dinner table devotions as it is for the "publish or perish" world of the university. We cannot begin to tackle everything. There's way too much for any one person to digest. Much of what we do chew on provides us only with empty intellectual calories. We must choose fare that does not just fill our brains, our time, or our research grant requirements. We should choose what truly nourishes us, that which our Shepherd puts on our plate.

God Signs at the Bottom Line (12:13-14)

So what did we learn from our rambles with Qoheleth down wisdom's paths? The editor boils it down to two closing verses for us:

Now all has been heard; here is the conclusion of the matter: Fear God and keep his commandments, for this is the whole [duty] of man. For God will bring every deed into judgment, including every hidden thing, whether it is good or evil.
(12:13-14)

Has the editor accurately captured the thrust of Qoheleth's message?

Many commentators doubt it. They argue that the Teacher's sharp critiques and bold investigations would never lead him to such a traditional and conservative message. The editor got it wrong, they claim—probably on purpose, because he could not tolerate Qoheleth's pessimism and blatant disregard for the sensitivities of the pious.

But is that really so? True, the Teacher sharply critiques and questions traditional wisdom in many instances. In contrast to his instructors he has many more (honest) questions than (only partially) honest answers (see 7:24). But does his keen insight and research really make him throw out the central concern of all Hebraic wisdom of that time: leading the people into obedient service to the God of the Covenant? Let's let Qoheleth himself speak on the issue:

To the man who pleases him, God gives wisdom, knowledge and happiness, but to the sinner he gives the task of gathering and storing up wealth to hand it over to the one who pleases God.
(2:26)

I know that whatever God does endures for ever; nothing can be added to it, nor anything taken from it; God has made it so, in order that men should fear before him.
(3:14 RSV)

God will bring to judgment both the righteous and the wicked, for there will be a time for every activity, a time for every deed.

(3:17)

For when dreams increase, empty words grow many: but do you fear God.

(5:7 RSV)

It is good to grasp the one and not to let go of the other. The man who fears God will avoid all extremes.

(7:18)

Although a wicked man commits a hundred crimes and still lives a long time, I know that it will go better with God-fearing men.

(8:12)

[I] concluded that the righteous and the wise and what they do are in God's hands. . . .

(9:1)

Follow the ways of your heart and whatever your eyes see, but know that for all these things God will bring you to judgment.

(11:9)

To be sure, Qoheleth raises many questions about the process by which God administers the world and its creatures. But he never calls into question the existence of an almighty, righteous God or our ability to be in a meaningful relationship to our Lord and Maker. In fact, our total dependence upon God for every good thing rules out living successfully without God. Qoheleth's doubts and questions never lead him onto the slippery slope of secularism. His questions come out of the context of a solid faith.

The editor's expansion of Qoheleth's own words "Fear God" to "Fear God and keep his commandments" (12:13) is fully in harmony with that message.

The editor adds: "for this is the whole man" (12:13). The Hebrew word for "duty," inserted by many translators, is entirely missing—and for good reason. Qoheleth's argument has been consistently that human beings cannot achieve anything lasting and that they themselves will disappear as "a breath." So we wonder, is there any substance to us at all?

The editor fills in Qoheleth's answer: Yes, of course! Our obedient relationship to God is not only our option. It is not only our duty. It is us! It is the very stuff of which we are made. The bottom line of our lives keeps adding up to that horribly frustrating zero no matter how we twist and turn—*unless we meet God there.* God turns the nil into an infinitely large number because through his goodness, our Lord makes us his own. To the world we may amount to nothing. To God we're priceless children, bought at the incredibly high cost of Jesus' blood.

At the muffler shop we're a somebody only for as long as it takes to tack a new muffler under the car. Beneath the sun we remain a somebody for seventy, maybe eighty years, and then we turn back to being a nobody. Only if God adopts us and remakes us in the image of Jesus can we honestly say that we remain a *somebody.* Our only hope of surviving the cruel, levelling injustice of death lies in finding lasting shelter in the heart of God.

In 12:14 the editor simply echoes Qoheleth's own words in 11:9. Although we cannot understand how, God remains on the throne and *will* put everything right. So enjoy!

Good Night!

The contented snores make Grandpa
chuckle as he shuffles to the door and
closes the book. Tomorrow brings a new
day when he'll read them an even better
one.